Lessons in Leadership 2.0 The Tough Stuff

Brick Tower Press
Habent Sua Fata Libelli

Manhanset House
Shelter Island Hts., New York 11965-0342

bricktower@aol.com • tech@absolutelyamazingebooks.com
• absolutelyamazingebooks.com

Library of Congress Cataloging-in-Publication Data
Adubato, Steve
Lessons in Leadership 2.0: The Tough Stuff.
p. cm.
1. BUSINESS & ECONOMICS / Leadership.
2. BUSINESS & ECONOMICS / Management.
3. BUSINESS & ECONOMICS / Industries / Media & Comminications.
Nonfiction, I. Title.
ISBN: 978-1-899694-08-2 Hardcover, 978-1-899694-17-4 Trade Paper

November 2023

Lessons in Leadership 2.0
The Tough Stuff

Steve Adubato, Ph.D.

Also by Steve Adubato

"Steve is an exceptional communicator and dynamic leadership coach who shares his best insights in this terrific new book. In these challenging times, it's more important than ever to hone your message, cut through the noise and inspire your teams. Steve is a master!"

—*Robert C. Garrett*
    CEO
    Hackensack Meridian Health

"Steve Adubato does a masterful job of uncovering many of the core principles that can lead to world class leadership. You will read and reread his book for years to come."

—*Michael Clinton*
    Author, ROAR Into the Second Half of Life

"Steve's new book will remind you that a leader is never done learning from their peers or employees...A 'must read' from a great leader."

—*Marjorie Perry*
    President & CEO
    MZM Construction & Management

"Steve Adubato shared such great insight in his first *Lessons in Leadership* book that I didn't think he had anything left to share. But, not surprisingly, he proved me wrong! I have always valued Steve's leadership advice, and this is a must read for anyone who leads people – or aspires to be a great leader."

—*Ira Robbins*
    CEO
    Valley Bank

"Steve's new book is engaging, thought-provoking and adaptable for any level of leader in every walk of life. His ability to disarm and, most importantly, build the readers' confidence to make a difference in their daily lives is unrivaled!!"

—*John Devin*
  President
  Fedway Associates

"I congratulate and commend Steve Adubato for sharing his leadership lessons in his new book. All of us in higher education and beyond can learn a lot from his wisdom."

—*Lamont O. Repollet, Ed.D.*
  President
  Kean University

"Steve Adubato is spot on...leadership is 'tough stuff', and how we handle it defines us as leaders. Thanks, Steve, for challenging us to consistently self-reflect and be conscious and authentic in the steps we take in response."

—*Michele N. Siekerka, Esq.*
  President & CEO
  New Jersey Business & Industry Association

"Once again, Steve Adubato provides existing and aspiring leaders with the insight and skills indispensable to navigating 21st century challenges, paired with the clarity of a seasoned and effective communicator."

—*Matthew Borowick*
  Vice President
  University Communications, Seton Hall University

"Steve has facilitated the IUOE Local 825 Leadership Academy for several years. *Lessons in Leadership 2.0: The Tough Stuff* is a huge part of the Academy's curriculum. This book and Steve's coaching has been transformative for our leaders. We see it every day. He has made a huge difference in our organization."

—*Greg Lalevee*
   Business Manager & General VP
   International Union of Operating Engineers Local 825

"Steve's book is filled with invaluable lessons on how genuine leadership continues to evolve in unpredictable ways, and strategies to navigate change with a solid foundation of emotional intelligence, stress management, and self-care."

—*Patricia Stark*
   Author of **Calmfidence,** *Radio & Television Broadcaster,*
   and Communications Trainer

"In this post-COVID era, leaders are being tested as never before, and Steve Adubato offers smart solutions to make any leader more effective."

—*Neal Shapiro*
   President & CEO
   The WNET Group (PBS)

"Steve's book is insightful and has many great tips on how to be a successful leader in today's changing and challenging landscape. I highly recommend the read!"

—*Glenn L. Friedman*
   CEO
   Prager Metis CPAs

"With *Lessons in Leadership 2.0: The Tough Stuff*...Steve Adubato has hit it out of the park once again. Leadership is not a destination, it's a journey. Great leaders are adept at fighter pilot like situational awareness, but also know that it's all about the long game and fully comprehending that the rules are ever changing. It's the tough stuff that Steve talks about!"

—*Dennis Wilson*
President & CEO
Delta Dental of New Jersey, Delta Dental of Connecticut

"Steve's new book provides what we all need to advance our personal leadership skills and help organizations reach new levels of success. His shared wisdom has helped our organization save and enhance more lives than ever before through organ and tissue donation and transplantation."

—*Carolyn M. Welsh*
President & CEO
NJ Sharing Network

"If you are on a never-ending quest to be a better leader, then Steve Adubato's *Lessons in Leadership 2.0: The Tough Stuff* is a must. Just when you thought you read all there was on the subject, Steve reinvigorates your mind with new ways of understanding the importance of leadership."

—*Jim Kirkos*
CEO
Meadowlands Chamber & CVB

"There is nothing more important in leadership than being an effective communicator. And there are few better communicators in the country than Steve Adubato. Steve's updated version of *Lessons in Leadership* including examples of learning from mistakes and facing new challenges reminds me of another important leadership attribute: candor. Steve's book will arm you with tools to tackle the ever-evolving nature of leading teams."

—*Wesley Mathews*
President & CEO
Choose New Jersey

"Steve Adubato has a unique gift...he can explain complicated and important concepts using straightforward, relatable Jersey-talk. He writes with candor, boldness, and good humor. Too many leadership books are filled with empty bromides, but Steve writes like a normal, smart person talks to his friends at the diner."

—*Elie Honig*
CNN Senior Legal Analyst, Bestselling Author, and Former Federal and State Prosecutor

"The value in Steve's lessons are not only their creative insights, but the ease to which they can be put into practical use for all styles of leaderships. His lessons are more than just conceptually insightful; they are useful in our daily leadership experiences."

—*Paul J. Di Maio*
General Counsel & Chief Administrative Officer
Delta Dental of New Jersey, Inc.
Delta Dental of Connecticut, Inc.

"I've known of Steve Adubato for a long time and have had the recent pleasure of getting to know him better. His knowledge on leadership and ways to improve communication are invaluable. He has used his platform to help people become stronger and more effective leaders. These lessons are ones that have an impact on those ready and willing to learn."

—*Patrick McVerry*
President & General Manager
Somerset Patriots, Double-A Affiliate of the New York Yankees

"Steve is a well-known and trusted leader in this space. In *Lessons in Leadership 2.0: The Tough Stuff*, Steve provides great insights on how leadership has evolved through these past few years of turbulence – and the resulting need for a more human-centered approach."

—*Tammy Garnes Mata*
Chief DEI Officer & Head of People Resources and Relations
Valley Bank

"Steve Adubato has helped our executive team and physicians elevate their leadership skills significantly. In *Lessons in Leadership 2.0: The Tough Stuff,* Steve continues to share great tips and tools to help leaders be decisive, communicate effectively and motivate their teams."

—*James Blazar*
   Chief Strategy Officer & Executive Vice President
   Hackensack Meridian Health

"Steve Adubato is a master communicator and in this masterful new book - *Lessons in Leadership 2.0: The Tough Stuff.* He gives extraordinary insight into leadership at all levels and invaluable advice to both experienced and aspiring leaders."

—*John Sarno*
   President
   Employers Association of NJ

"Effective leadership requires a daunting range of attributes, and in his new book, *Lessons in Leadership 2.0: The Tough Stuff,* Dr Adubato explores the critical elements of leadership and how great leaders succeed in mastering them."

—*Gil Medina*
   Senior Real Estate Executive

"Leaders that follow Steve Adubato's books have valuable insight into leadership from any position in the organization. If you want to increase your personal value, this is a must read. Mastering even one component of Dr. Adubato's strategies will positively impact your leadership style. It's the reason why we ask Steve to train our leaders at Kessler Foundation."

—*Rodger L. DeRose*
   President & CEO
   Kessler Foundation

"*Lessons in Leadership 2.0: The Tough Stuff* is current, impactful, and practical. Working with Steve Adubato and reading his books have become invaluable tools to me as a leader and to our firm as we develop new leaders. I highly recommend both!"

—*Lori A. Roth, CPA*
Global Managing Partner
Prager Metis CPAs

"Steve Adubato is a pro! My hat goes off to him because there are only a few great communicators around...and he is one of the best!"

—*Suze Orman*
Financial Guru & New York Times *Bestselling Author*

"Steve provides a roadmap to navigate the strategic leadership filled with actionable insights and real word examples."

—*Linda McHugh, MBA, MT*
EVP, Chief Experience & People Officer
Hackensack Meridian Health

"Leadership is one of those things that everyone thinks they can do or that some are naturally born to do. As Steve points out, leadership is learned, studied, and quite intentional. *Lessons in Leadership 2.0: The Tough Stuff*, is an inspirational read that dives into the nuts and bolts of leadership by focusing on the real work that self-aware leaders undertake to inspire others to perform at the highest level. Bravo Steve!"

—*Joe Lee*
Vice President & General Manager
NJ PBS

"Once again, Steve expertly presents the essential role leadership plays in achieving consistent performance. He persuasively underscores the strong relationship between learning and leadership. In these complex and challenging times, *Lessons in Leadership 2.0: The Tough Stuff* is a must read for every leader and an insightful, informative, and engaging roadmap to developing the exceptional leadership skills necessary to succeed in the future."

—*Larry Downes*
Retired Chairman
New Jersey Resources

"Steve Adubato brings a fresh perspective to leadership in these ever-changing times. This book offers solid and practical tools to be an effective leader and a powerful reminder that authentic leadership emerges from honest communication with the self."

—*Renée Marino*
Communication Expert, TEDx Speaker & Best-Selling Author of **Becoming a Master Communicator**

"*Lessons in Leadership 2.0: The Tough Stuff* is a must read for anyone in a leadership or management role or for anyone looking to improve themselves. How one leads is a continuing educational endeavor and Steve shares his insights and experiences which allows the reader to build on his or her style which will lead to continued success"

—*Anthony Russo*
President
Commerce and Industry Association of New Jersey
CEO/Publisher, **COMMERCE** *Magazine*

"Steve Adubato is the ultimate 'code breaker' when it comes to making people 'look in the mirror' and honestly reflect upon what they need to change or improve upon in order to become a stronger and more effective leader."

—*Timothy Hogan, FACHE*
Executive VP
Care Transformation Services, Hackensack Meridian Health
President & Chief Hospital Executive
Riverview Medical Center

"Leadership is all about making tough decisions, but never losing focus on the values that you represent. Whether it's in life or business, leadership is needed and being able to discuss that topic with Steve and Mary is absolutely amazing. I'm very thankful for being able to be a guest on their show and learning as well."

—*Eric LeGrand*
Motivational Speaker, Sports Analyst, Philanthropist & Entrepreneur
bELieve 52

"Most of us are artful dodgers of situations that make us uncomfortable, Steve is absolutely right that "artful confrontation" is a skill that great leaders possess and develop over time to make the 'tough stuff' less tough."

—*Randy Stodard*
Chief Marketing Officer
Delta Dental of New Jersey, Delta Dental of Connecticut

"Steve thoughtfully recognizes the element of wellness-centered leadership that is so critical in this day and age. He offers practical ways for successful leaders to tend to themselves while caring for their teams."

—*Amy Frieman, MD, MBA, FAAHPM*
President
Physician Alliance, Hackensack Meridian Health

"Steve Adubato always has a refreshing take on the events of the day. His voice brings clarity to confusion and his passion produces more light than heat."

—*Jim Bell*
Former Executive Producer
The TODAY Show, *NBC*

"At a time when business executives are facing unprecedented challenges, Steve provides a post-COVID look at what it means to be a great leader. From 'connecting the dots' to discussing the 'tough stuff,' this book shares insight that is valuable for veteran leaders to those just starting out, and everyone in between."

—*Francis J. Giantomasi*
Co-Chair, Executive Committee
Chiesa Shahinian & Giantomasi PC

"In his latest book, Steve continues his insightful exploration of the characteristics of a great leader, particularly in a post-COVID world. Importantly, Steve delves into the open, honest and frank discussions leaders must have to attract and retain the best talent in a given industry. Brilliant work! A must-read!"

—*Thomas P. Scrivo*
Managing Partner
O'Toole Scrivo, Certified Civil Trial Attorney by the Supreme Court of New Jersey

"Leadership is hard- especially in today's climate with so many evolving social, legal and political challenges. Steve's wisdom – gleaned from years of conversations with some of the most dynamic and inspiring leaders of our time – will help any leader work through 'the tough stuff' in their role. It provides a myriad of perspectives on how to successfully navigate an ever-changing work landscape through supportive, sensitive and professional approaches that help create positive and impactful leaders and organizations—making a constructive difference in their community."

—*Michael Schmidt*
    Executive Director & CEO
    The Healthcare Foundation of New Jersey

"Steve is a gifted communicator and brilliant strategist. When I'm trying to evaluate whether a leader has made the correct decision, in the face of a seemingly impossible situation, I find myself asking, 'What would Steve do?' This book finally answers many of those questions. The irony which we're all living in today is that at a time when the country is in greater need than ever of wise leadership, it seems in short supply. This book is a great step in increasing that supply."

—*Frank Morano*
    Radio Talk Show, WABC Radio

Dedication

This book is dedicated to leaders of all stripes who work every day to make a difference and inspire others to do the same. A special dedication goes to all those leaders on the "front lines" who since March 2020—when COVID-19 became all too real—committed themselves to helping others. I'm talking about physicians, nurses, respiratory therapists, public health workers, first responders and those who helped COVID patients (some of whom didn't survive) and their families navigate incredibly unpredictable and terrifying times.

In addition, this book is dedicated to all the leaders on the "front lines" who didn't have the luxury of working remotely or taking time off. These leaders managed or worked in our supermarkets, convenience stores, public transportation, sanitation, and mail and package delivery. Whether they call themselves "leaders" or not, that is exactly who they are. Let's never forget their sacrifice and service that made life for the rest of us more manageable because of what they did. All the leaders highlighted in this dedication were knee-deep in the "tough stuff" this book explores. There are no words that could appropriately thank them.

Acknowledgments

Writing a book—even if it is your sixth, is always challenging. No author does it alone. You need a lot of help and support, not to mention guidance, feedback, and sometimes push back. Enter Mary Gamba, my colleague and partner professionally for over two decades. She's my confidant, my consigliere (think *The Godfather*), and colleague who kept this writing process on track, focused, and on time. She questioned and challenged the value of every chapter in this book, constantly considering the impact we needed to have on our audience, including all leaders who face a lot of "tough stuff" in these very challenging and uncertain times. It is hard to appropriately thank Mary for her contribution to *Lessons in Leadership 2.0: The Tough Stuff*. It is a much better book because of her input, insight, and leadership.

I also want to thank our editor Barry Cohen, Managing Member, AdLab Media Communications, LLC, and our publisher, John T. Colby Jr., Brick Tower Press. I have to thank my colleagues at both the Caucus Educational Corporation, our not-for-profit production company affiliated with public broadcasting, as well as the terrific team behind the scenes on our "Lessons in Leadership" podcast that Mary and I are proud to co-host. I have learned from every one of these teammates to be a better leader. Their feedback, sometimes hard to hear, has been greatly appreciated—especially when my leadership (and communication style) has fallen short of what I preach in this book. And, to all the leaders who have joined Mary and I on the "Lessons in Leadership" podcast, I say thank you for sharing your wisdom and insight. We have learned so much from you.

I also want to thank the clients of *Stand & Deliver* who I am honored to coach, teach, and learn from when it comes to the art of leadership. Facilitating leadership seminars, both in person and remotely, is still greatly rewarding. Being an executive coach and advising dozens of dedicated and talented leaders is also extremely gratifying. Doing what you love every day is a gift. Yes, of course it's work, but it also brings much joy and satisfaction, which I try not to take for granted. To the companies and organizations that have retained our firm Stand & Deliver to coach their leaders, you have my gratitude and loyalty.

Finally, I want to thank my family. My wife Jennifer and our three children, Nick, Chris, and Olivia, as well as my older son, Stephen. I can only hope that my children grow to become not just strong and confident leaders, but really good and caring people who make a difference in the world. Because, ultimately, making a difference is really what leadership is all about.

Table of Contents

Foreword

I have had the privilege and honor to have worked shoulder to shoulder with Dr. Steve Adubato for almost 25 years. When I first began my professional journey, I could not have imagined that one day I would be the executive director of our non-profit television production company, the Caucus Educational Corporation (founded by Steve in 1994), and President for our leadership and communication firm, Stand & Deliver. While Steve has been an executive coach and mentor to so many, he has done the same for me, often providing that hard-to-hear feedback that has helped me grow into the confident and successful leader I am today.

When Steve came to me and said, "Hey, I have this idea. I want to write a follow-up to *Lessons in Leadership*," I couldn't have been more excited about the idea. And then we he asked me to contribute to the content, it meant the world to me, since we have grown so much professionally and personally throughout our journey together. I was confident that what we had to share would be extremely valuable to every leader, regardless of where they fit in an organizational chart.

It was in early summer of 2020, and about 4-months into the COVID-19 pandemic. While there had been so many lessons learned in the time since Steve published *Lessons in Leadership* in 2016, the leadership lessons from just those few months after the start of the pandemic multiplied exponentially. Due to social distancing and most of the world coming to a screeching halt, there was a new way of leading, communicating, coaching, mentoring, and running meetings. Along with countless other organizations, we pivoted and embraced virtual platforms such as Zoom and Microsoft Teams to stay connected with our key stakeholders as well as our team. But we quickly learned that technology alone wasn't enough to ensure the viability and success of our organizations. It was going to take grit, innovation, and resilience to navigate the months, and ultimately years, of the pandemic. Leaders had to find new ways of building relationships while also managing to recruit, train and retain a talented team, all while dealing with the reality of burnout and the "wellness-leadership connection". The truly exceptional leaders embraced the reality that they needed to take a more strategic approach to navigating their organization through the pandemic, while letting go of the status quo and expecting excellence from themselves and their teams.

Fast forward to today, 3 ½ years after Steve had the idea to write this book, and the lessons he shares in the chapters that follow address all of those leadership areas and more, and are just as relevant whether you are leading your organization through a pandemic, an acquisition or a merger, or any other monumental event that challenges you as a leader. I feel truly blessed to have had Steve as my coach, mentor, and friend for so many years, and I am confident that the tips and tools he leaves behind in this book are invaluable for all leaders. Happy reading.

Mary Gamba
President, Stand & Deliver
Executive Director, Caucus Educational Corporation

Introduction

I'm fascinated with leadership. I'm constantly trying to understand why a particular leader handles a situation one way while another takes a very different approach. Why are some leaders better equipped to face a crisis, obstacle, or challenge while others panic and fold under the pressure? Why are certain leaders constantly innovating, reinventing, and pivoting while others cling to the "status quo" as if this "status quo" is ever good enough? And the age-old question...are great leaders born or can you really teach this leadership stuff?

There are so many different ways of thinking about leadership and, yes, so many books on the topic. It's funny, when I wrote my last book, *Lessons in Leadership* published in 2016, it was cathartic on many levels. It forced me to express how I viewed leadership in its many forms at that particular time. More importantly, that book has served as a template for much of my leadership coaching, commentary, seminars, and teaching and caused me to challenge and sometimes question my own leadership approach involving the two organizations I oversee. (The Caucus Educational Corporation, a non-profit production company with programming airing on public television, and Stand & Deliver, our communication and leadership coaching firm.) It has also provided jumping off points for compelling conversations with my colleague Mary Gamba on our weekly podcast, "Lessons in Leadership," on which Mary co-anchors and serves as executive producer.

The Best Leaders Are Always Evolving

So, many years since I sat down to write the original, *Lessons in Leadership* why another leadership book? One reason is that I have learned many new "lessons" about leadership during that time. (Mostly because of my making new mistakes, facing new challenges, as well as experiencing some leadership breakthroughs over the past 7-plus years.) I've also come to the realization that my view of leadership has evolved significantly during this time. I'm not so convinced that the so-called "lessons" and assumptions I wrote about in my last book are so rock solid anymore. One size definitely does not fit all. As I said, my thinking about leadership—particularly exceptional, strategic and innovative leadership—has not only been impacted by my experiences and challenges as a leader, but also those faced by the leaders I've studied, coached and interviewed over many years. Further, in 2023, the world feels more complex, confusing and yes, scary, at times. At the very least, we can all acknowledge that today's leaders must navigate in a much more unpredictable environment including a multi-year, ever-evolving, global pandemic that has impacted virtually every aspect of our lives.

In many ways, exceptional leadership seems harder than ever. It requires a diverse and nimble skillset, an unprecedented degree of self-confidence and self-reflection, not to mention a healthy dose of "emotional intelligence." Exceptional leadership not only takes the ability to empathize with team members (including the often-difficult task of balancing and integrating our work responsibilities with those at home and in our often-complex personal lives) but the awareness that we as leaders and as individuals must take better care of ourselves in order to be and feel our best—especially under such trying conditions. (See this book's chapter on The Wellness-Leadership Connection.)

So, what exactly is the so-called leadership "tough stuff" that I refer to in the title of this book? One of the books that had a significant impact on me is, *Don't Sweat the Small Stuff*, by the late Dr. Richard Carlson. Dr. Carlson would later publish a follow up book entitled *What About the Big Stuff* in 2002. So why not *Lessons in Leadership 2.0: What About the Tough Stuff*? My effort to discuss the leadership "tough stuff" is a nod to Dr. Carlson's acknowledgement that there are some challenges that go beyond the "small stuff." So, what "tough stuff" can readers expect to be explored in the pages that follow? Try these; "Why Feedback is a Funny Thing." Simply put, why it is so difficult for so many leaders to give and receive constructive, candid, and hard to hear feedback? Further, why it is more important than ever for leaders to understand the importance of giving and receiving constructive feedback. Easier said than done, I know, that is why I call it the "tough stuff."

We will also explore "strategic leadership," which often requires what I call, "connecting the dots." It's not enough for leaders to simply put one foot in front of the other and move forward in a linear fashion—or wait for direction from their "boss". Exceptional, strategic leaders need to be more visionary, proactive, and innovative than ever, not exactly predicting the future but rather anticipating certain events, trends, outcomes and market forces and conditions—including the ongoing impact, challenges and, yes, opportunities created by COVID-19 and other major "disruptions."

Or, what about "strategic micromanagement?" That's right. In the original *Lessons in Leadership,* I talked about the need for us as leaders to more effectively "delegate" more to members of our team. I still believe that, but I've come to realize and embrace the reality that not all micromanagement is overbearing, poor leadership—even if you have delegated a specific task. In fact, I make the case in this book that if leaders micromanage in a more strategic, thoughtful and intentional manner, they can be more effective and productive, which will help develop and coach those they delegate to. And yes, at times it's not only appropriate but required that leaders "get into the weeds" when it comes to executing a plan.

In *Lessons in Leadership 2.0,* I also explore what I call, "artful confrontation." I'm talking about the ability and willingness of leaders to have difficult, but necessary, conversations about organizational realities including underperforming team members, a situational crisis, fiscal problems and thorny challenges and obstacles that must be confronted and dealt with directly. Many leaders I've coached, as well as some leaders reading this book, say they "don't like confrontation." I get it, except that tired cliché and attitude will not help you or your organization move forward and deal with difficult and pressing situations, market conditions and decisions that must be addressed. Yes, that's "confrontation," but it must be done in an artful, thoughtful and respectful manner as opposed to simply being confrontational because some leaders just seem to enjoy conflict and controversy.

More tough stuff...As you will see in the pages that follow, I am also big on leaders actively and enthusiastically engaging team members and other key stakeholders. I use the term "forced engagement" in this book and attempt to make the case that as leaders, we can't simply hope, pray or wish that our people will become more engaged, but rather we must take certain actions and create a dynamic and welcoming communication environment where engagement is not an option but is required. It is necessary to gain the perspective and insight from those around you and motivate them to feel more a "part of the team". That's right, leaders must sometimes "force" this type of engagement, but do it in a safe, supportive, and collegial environment. If they can't or won't, the silence coming back can be deafening and dangerous. Actively engaging team members and other key stakeholders is even more important as we communicate more and more on "remote" platforms—a subject we delve into with an eye toward strengthening our ability to navigate the virtual world.

Wellness and Relationship-Building Must Be Intentional

In addition, *Lessons in Leadership 2.0* will explore "strategic relationship building." Ask yourself; "what exactly is my approach as a leader to establishing and maintaining relationships with key people in my universe?" Many leaders I have coached tell me such relationship-building "just happens" or they "do it on an as-hoc or as-needed basis." This approach to relationship building can be haphazard and can be overly transactional. I say, meaningful professional (as well as certain personal) relationships must be nurtured and developed and nurtured in a strategic, consistent, and genuinely thoughtful fashion. It would be great if they simply happened "organically," but most don't. Therefore, in this book I will explore what I call the "hub and spokes" strategic relationship building model which I am confident will be helpful for you as a reader and leader.

Our book will also explore what my friend and colleague Greg Lalevee, Business Manager for IUOE Local 825, calls "leaky bags of sh*t." What are these so-called "leaky bags?" Simply put, they are problems that get dumped in your lap as a leader from team members and others who see you as a "Mr. / Ms. Fix It" leader whose job it is to clean up every mess, every time. Sure, at times this is exactly what we do as leaders—we solve problems and fix them. But such a "leaky bag" culture can be problematic, and this particular chapter will explore the need for leaders to coach and develop team members to think more strategically and creatively. Every team member should be able to "connect dots" and identify potential solutions when challenges arise as opposed to simply handing them off or yes, dumping them on your desk just because you sit at the top of the organizational chart. The best leaders don't encourage a "leaky bag" culture, but rather a "let's all consider our options" mentality.

One of my favorite chapters is called, "Don't Sweat the Q&A" in which I explore the fact that many leaders experience unhealthy anxiety and unnecessary fear around challenging questions they are often asked after and/or during a presentation they make to a particularly important and challenging audience. This is often called the Q&A portion of a meeting or public forum that can be extremely stressful. But it doesn't have to be this way. This chapter explores a more concrete, practical and very strategic approach to think about, and prepare for any question you get asked no matter how difficult or how potentially adversarial the questioner. It's about seeing the Q&A as an opportunity to clarify, connect with and engage the most difficult and skeptical audience as well as being open to new and more innovative ways of addressing the issue or change you have proposed. As the late "60 Minutes" reporter Mike Wallace, known as an extremely challenging interviewer, once said, "There are no embarrassing questions. There are only embarrassing answers." I couldn't agree more.

Lessons in Leadership 2.0 also explores the concept of "extreme ownership," which comes from the book, *Extreme Ownership: How U.S. Navy SEALs Lead and Win,* written by Navy Seals Jocko Willink and Leif Babin. In this chapter, I use a case study from the late General Colin Powell who served as Secretary of State and was considered to be a giant in American military leadership. We explore General Powell's much publicized and internationally embarrassing testimony before the United Nations in 2003 when making the case for the United States going to war with Iraq because of him claiming, on behalf of the then Bush administration, that Iraq had "weapons of mass destruction." General Powell's testimony was in fact incorrect and flawed, which in turn had deadly implications during the U.S. war with Iraq. To his credit, General Powell took full responsibility for his faulty testimony. He didn't blame, scapegoat or finger point. He owned it. He owned all of it in a very extreme fashion. In this book, I'll make the case that such "extreme ownership" and taking of full responsibility continues to be all too rare for leaders of every stripe—yet clearly an important and admirable leadership trait.

We will also explore the connection between wellness and leadership. I'm talking about our own wellbeing as well as our responsibility as leaders to create a "culture of wellness," which involves not only tangible actions we can take as leaders to promote a positive culture, but also encouraging fellow team members to incorporate wellness into their leadership toolkit and mindset. In a post-pandemic environment, our wellbeing, as well as that of every team member, is more important than ever.

Retirement?
The Great Resignation... and Is Everyone Really a Leader?

Lessons in Leadership 2.0 will also take on the question of retirement. Why write about retirement in a book about leadership "lessons?" For me and many other leaders, the question of retirement has become a very different matter, especially since COVID. In this chapter, I will examine how "working from home" (for me much of that is walking to our third floor with two broadcast studios, one of which I use for our remote seminars and coaching, often wearing very casual attire) or working off of my iPhone from just about anywhere. No, it's not as effective as being "in person," but it's so convenient. This has impacted much of my thinking about how long I can and even want to do this kind of work. To be clear, I still do some in-person seminars, on-location broadcasting, and have select client and business-associate in-person meetings, but most of my work is done remotely. Instead of seeing retirement as a black and white "final" decision, this chapter explores the importance of workers "refiring," as Ken Blanchard and Morton Shaevitz state in their book, *Refire! Don't Retire.* Yes, continually challenging and motivating yourself as a leader to contribute and make a difference—that is a major reason why I decided to write this sixth book on leadership and communication. I'm trying to refire all the time. When I stop wanting to "refire," I guess I will retire!

The irony of including a chapter on "The Great Resignation," along with a chapter on retirement, is not lost on me. Many professionals have decided to resign and move in a different direction or take a new path from the job they are currently in. I'm not talking "giving up" or "giving in," but rather the reality that a global pandemic, and other lifechanging events, cause many to reevaluate their lives and make major changes. Simply put, as leaders of organizations, we are losing some really talented team members. In this chapter, I express how in the early stages of the pandemic, how tough it was to lose several talented team members in a short period of time—including a top-level colleague who worked shoulder to shoulder with Mary in our production company. As leaders, we must face the stark reality that retaining our best team members is a never-ending effort—with no guarantees. There are times and situations that no matter what we do as leaders—some of our employees will leave anyway. That is really "tough stuff."

Finally, *Lessons in Leadership 2.0: The Tough Stuff* takes on the complex question, "Is everyone really a leader?" In this chapter, I argue that in order to be a high-performing team, everyone on your team in one way or another must be a leader in certain situations, regardless of their job title or description. I'm convinced that team members "just doing their job" or "staying in their lane" will only guarantee at best that the status quo will prevail. In a highly competitive world, that often means that we are frequently moving backward. In these challenging times, this "status quo" approach won't help your team thrive. COVID, 9/11, the horrific number of school shootings, and other crises or events have taught us that in certain circumstances, titles matter only so much, and that some team members must step up and lead (or not) because that's what's needed. Yet, beyond such extraordinary and tragic events and circumstances, our everyday tough challenges and ever-changing environment (just think technology advancements) often requires that everyone on our team must lead.

Together with my colleague, Mary Gamba, who has contributed to this work in so many ways, it is my sincere hope that *Lessons in Leadership 2.0: What About the Tough Stuff?* provides you with practical, strategic, and applicable tools and tips to help you more effectively navigate increasingly choppy and uncertain leadership waters. I'm confident that the examples, anecdotes and mini-case studies in this book will be recognizable and relevant to you. On a selfish note, writing this book— my 6th on leadership with a heavy dose of communication-related content—has challenged me to think long and hard about what I truly believe as well as practice. It has challenged me to be even more painfully honest and self-reflective as to whether I'm actually doing as a leader what I am recommending that you do. Let's just say, after a lot of effort and good intentions, it is a mixed bag. Like you, I am a work in progress, as I'm still practicing to be the best leader I can be.

Finally, to paraphrase a very wise person (I'm not actually sure who said it) who once said "Practice doesn't make perfect. Rather, practice makes progress." As leaders, let's make some progress...together!

Chapter 1
Is Everyone "Really" a Leader?

I've long believed that everyone on a team MUST be a leader for the team to reach its potential. At the same time, I've often been frustrated when one team member or another "doesn't take the lead" on a project, initiative or challenge facing our organization. In my most frustrated moments, I've said to Mary (a real leader) on occasion, "Why is it that we have to tell 'Jane' what needs to be done? We need Jane to lead and take the initiative."

Mary, who is extremely levelheaded, has often responded by telling me, "Everyone has their role...as long as they get the job done...it's okay." Over the years, we have discussed, and sometimes debated, the issue of leadership and asked the question, "So, is everyone *really* a leader?" Or, can our or any organization or team succeed at the highest level of excellence with team members just doing their job within narrow parameters or doing what they are directed to do?

On a Great Team...Everyone Must Lead...In Some Way

I've been in leadership positions long enough to know that this is not a black and white question. At one time or another, all of us must follow the lead of others. And yet, I still struggle with this complex topic. I have come to believe that to be a truly great team, every team member must step up—must take the lead—must not hang back and wait for direction. To be clear, I'm not talking about an average or mediocre organization or team—I'm talking about an exceptional team with very high standards—or a team that aspires to become an exceptional one.

Let's add another perspective to this discussion. Enter our longtime friend Larry Downes, former CEO at NJ Resources, who became a CEO of this major energy company at the age of 37. While he retired a couple of years ago, he is still an active philanthropist and student of leadership who speaks extensively on the topic, serving on many boards of non-profit organizations. In one of my many conversations with Larry over the years about leadership, he said, "Steve, everyone IS a leader." In fact, Larry joined Mary and me on our Lessons in Leadership podcast and said the following, "The way each individual performs, and no matter what they do, no matter how large or small, is the difference between the organization's success and failure. It is not about titles. Once you get your team members to embrace the fact that yes, they are leaders, people begin to think differently about themselves and their role in the organization. I strongly believe that everyone IS a leader."

Mary's View of "Leadership" Has Evolved...A lot

Larry raises some valid points. In fact, his argument (and my constant harping on this topic for over two decades) about everyone being a leader has apparently influenced Mary's thinking on the issue with her recently saying, "Nearly a decade ago, when we first had this conversation with Larry, I was cynical, thinking we need 'doers' who take direction from the top. Firsthand I have seen that this approach, having a team that is passive and simply waiting for instruction, is not sustainable. Success takes ownership and leadership from every level of an organization, and if you don't expect that of your team, they won't expect it of themselves."

Now consider high-pressure leadership by people who choose to lead in challenging, and in some cases, matters of life and death. It's often situational or connected to a crisis or unexpected event. Think 9/11. Imagine how courageous countless individuals were who stepped up to "lead" helping to save others' lives, attempting to bring them to safety through smoke-filled stairwells in the World Trade Center. These people were not told to be leaders; they didn't have a title with leadership in it. They just stepped up because their leadership was needed. That's an extraordinary and terribly painful example of what we mean by "everyone is a leader" or needs to be a leader in certain kinds of crises or unexpected events where titles, positions and an organizational hierarchy have no value.

Conversely, consider the horrible tragedy in Uvalde, Texas, where a crazed gunman entered an elementary school classroom and started shooting randomly. Now, picture all those law enforcement professionals with rank and leadership titles who stayed in the school hallway for over an hour and did nothing. No one stepped up. No one led, no one said we need to go in now. They stood on ceremony, title, and rank, while the highest ranking "leader" directed everyone to stand back for some ungodly reason. I'm not saying it was easy and I'm not sure what I would have done, but those were law enforcement professionals and leaders in title and rank who didn't step up while those heroes on 9/11, both in the World Trade Center and those who heroically on Flight 93 who pronounced, "Let's roll," pushed their way into the cockpit to attempt to save the lives of fellow passengers and lost their lives to terrorists / hijackers intending to do deadly harm.

Team Members Waiting to be "Told What to Do" Won't Work Anymore

As I often say to our leadership coaching clients; "I make suggestions...I have opinions, but you make decisions." Everyone on your team should be a leader if, as I've stated, that team is going to maximize its potential and truly achieve excellence. However, in many instances, I have seen too many professionals who simply choose to not take the initiative and not lead when the need or opportunity is right in front of them. I've worked with and coached many team members who appear to be comfortable and quite satisfied with still "waiting to be told what to do." Sure, I have seen glimpses of assertive and proactive leadership, the kind that involves taking the initiative and saying something like this; "You know, Steve and Mary, I was thinking, we need to do XYZ in order to improve how we are handling ABC. So, I propose that we..."

However, on too many teams, those instances are too rare. I've often said to Mary that, "I (or any official organizational leader) shouldn't be the one who too often identifies an issue, problem, or opportunity..." My point is that I struggle with why certain team members lack what I call a "leadership mindset."

My wife Jen has challenged me on this way of thinking by saying, "You don't get it. You created an organization and your team members do their job. You expect everyone to be 'all in' the way you are. That's not realistic and it's not fair." Jen argues this especially for 'younger people' in an organization who are just trying to figure out what they want to do. Who knows, Jen may be right, but I see real leadership as caring enough about your organization or team to see the need and/or opportunity to make things better and in turn saying, "I'm not going to wait until 'the boss' tells me we need to do whatever. I am going to take the initiative." I'm not saying that certain team members who simply "do their job" as defined in their list of job responsibilities don't care. Not at all. Rather, I am saying to be a real leader, as I define it, you must care more than "just doing your job" within the narrow confines of your assigned responsibilities.

This kind of leadership, which is often situational, requires that employees "get outside their comfort zone" and into a more proactive and assertive mindset about what they do and how they do it. Truly great teams and organizations don't succeed because team members accept the status quo. But the real question may be, "is everyone really capable of that kind of leadership, or are there other forms of leadership that don't require this assertive, innovative and highly entrepreneurial mindset?"

I've come to believe that much of one's leadership quotient is innate, based largely on a person's personality, upbringing, and level of ambition and commitment to real excellence. Mary and I have also seen team members who originally did not show this type of leadership, but when challenged and motivated, embraced the opportunity to play a larger, more impactful, leadership role. To be fair, we've had team members, and I've coached numerous clients and participants in our Stand & Deliver Leadership Academy, who consistently "take charge" and exhibit a high degree of energy and passion around not just how they perform but about the team's overall success. They want to be challenged. They challenge themselves. They initiate. They make suggestions in meetings and speak up without me or Mary (as official leaders) having to "force" their engagement and participation. At times, they have challenged me— questioning the value or strategic impact of one of my recommendations or proposed initiatives. *That's leadership.* Others, however, are much more passive. They hang back. They don't say very much. They don't question, challenge, or propose very much. My conclusion is that many of these professionals are simply "keeping their head down", incapable or unwilling to lead, which has a negative impact on even the best led organizations or teams.

So, after all this, is everyone really a leader? And is this even realistic or fair to expect of every team member? I've shared my thinking on this complex and multi-faceted leadership topic. Now, I'm asking you to consider how you view your role on your team and if you really want to lead in the way I've described. With this important question in mind, consider what I believe to be the traits of truly great leadership, regardless of where you fit on the organizational chart:

Step up and speak out. Easier said than done, I know. But really great leaders step up, are proactive and assertive, and share their perspective on a particular situation, circumstance, challenge or opportunity. Don't wait to be asked. I call it being "strategically assertive,'" which means you pick your spots, but hanging back consistently and rarely, if ever, sharing your thoughts, denies the organization / team of the benefit of your thinking.

Take the initiative. It's not just speaking up, but it is about taking action as well. If you see an opportunity to do things better, more efficiently, and with greater impact, take the initiative to not just share your thoughts, and be willing to propose some specifics as to how the team can move this initiative forward.

Promote a culture of coaching and leadership. It's not enough that you see yourself as a strong, assertive leader, but it is also critical that every team member understands from what you say and what you do that you not only expect them to step up and lead, but you want and need them to do this. Take the time to coach and mentor others to improve and reach their leadership potential.

Recognize team members. Create coaching and development opportunities for people to gain additional coaching and leadership tools. Praise their leadership and yes, reward it, with tangible benefits—including more money, perks, flexibility, etc.

Push back and challenge. As always, do it respectfully and frame it as an opportunity to consider another point of view. Of course, pick your spots. Be strategic, but don't accept the status quo, because "it is just the way we've always done things."

Get outside of your comfort zone, or as I like to say, "get comfortable being uncomfortable." That's right, the best leaders force themselves to try and do things that they may not be familiar or comfortable with. It's one thing to be pushed or encouraged to do this, but quite another to be proactive in doing it yourself. Staying comfortable all the time may feel safe and secure (in many situations—I'm a creature of habit) but it also makes it hard to grow and reach your full potential as a leader.

Give feedback to team members. Sometimes our coaching clients say they don't offer honest feedback or advice to their peers or colleagues because, "It's just not my place." They talk about "staying in their lane." In many cases, this approach makes sense. But if a colleague or peer needs help, offer help and advice. Sure, they may push back, they may even think you should mind your own business, but if you never offer, how would you ever know? The best leaders help other people. They take the risk of offering feedback even if it is not asked for. I didn't say it was easy, but we are not talking mediocre leadership here, but rather exceptional leaders and excellent teams. So, in the end, is everyone really a leader? No. But should they be? Clearly, yes.

Chapter 2
Change, Innovate, Adapt...Or Die: The Case of NJN

In 2010, I had a conversation with then NJ Governor Chris Christie about public broadcasting in our state. The PBS station in the Garden State was called New Jersey Network (NJN) and had been around for 41 years. The network had been receiving $11 million annually directly built into the state budget and millions of additional dollars that came from individual state departments and agencies. NJN had become heavily dependent on this huge public subsidy to keep its lights on and its studios open.

To disclose, Governor Christie and I had an interesting relationship and history up to this point. We were friendly, but there were several times when in interviewing him, things got especially testy, and he was less than enamored with me. The way I saw it, I was doing my job and he was doing his, but we had different styles. Yet, Governor Chris Christie was always candid and told you how he saw things—a quality that I always appreciated about him—even when I disagreed with his policies or his approach.

But that phone conversation in 2010 wasn't about any interview, a policy issue, or our respective personalities. It was about the future of NJN and the fact that Governor Christie had intended to eliminate the $11 million plus in state subsidies that the network so desperately depended upon to survive. Other New Jersey governors had floated the idea of significantly cutting, if not eliminating, state funding to NJN, but they always backed off. At least two of those governors had reached out to me directly to discuss the media landscape in New Jersey and what impact I thought it would have if NJN was broken off from state government. One of the biggest reasons for past governors backing off was the intense opposition to such a bold move from a New Jersey governor from the New Jersey Communications Workers of America (NJ CWA), the public workers union that represented approximately 130 NJN employees.

There had been talk for years about breaking NJN off the state government and making it an independent nonprofit entity, but it wound up being just that, talk. No real action. In the past, certain leaders at NJN had thrown out the idea of breaking away from state government—but those ideas never materialized. No leadership that took the initiative to make that happen. Without it being publicly stated, the philosophy with many at NJN seemed to be, let's just hope that things stay the same. Let's just keep the "status quo."

Leading Change Requires Courage and Confidence

Clearly one of the major challenges with becoming an independent entity, outside of state government, would be that the network would have to be a lot more entrepreneurial. It would have to be run like a business. NJN was raising some money through its foundation, but not nearly enough to sustain its operation. It would have to bring in more revenue and cut expenses, becoming more efficient and streamlined at producing, broadcasting, and promoting programming. Yet, the media environment in New Jersey and the nation was evolving rapidly. The internet was becoming an increasingly important information and news source. In addition, other commercial news outlets based in New Jersey were producing and airing a lot of NJ-centric content. Many legislators and prominent leaders in state government were questioning why New Jersey state government was in the media business when there were so many other private, independent media and information outlets. An additional point to consider is that New Jersey has long-suffered from not having a prominent media presence or identity. In fact, many New Jerseyans in the north have relied on New York media, while those in the southern part of the state have consumed Philadelphia media.

Change = Opposition

These much-needed changes at NJN also never happened because the CWA fought it, saying its primary concern was about its 130 employees that could potentially lose their jobs. Again, without publicly stating it, the strategy seemed to be among the most influential voices, let's just keep the status quo at NJN. No significant changes in the organizational model and definitely let's remain part of state government where taxpayer dollars will continue to flow in and largely help pay our bills, not to mention pay our members.

To quote the official CWA spokesperson from 2010 when Christie's proposal to eliminate NJN became public; "Frankly, the part about self-sustaining—that you will find the money somewhere else—that is a ridiculous thing to say in this environment." The CWA representative went on to say that without state support, the network's news and public affairs programs would be gutted; "I just don't see how the news program continues, at least the way it is now. It's hard to see what they'll do besides replay PBS stuff."

Only one catch—I knew Governor Christie and he wasn't simply threatening to cut state funding and eliminate NJN as other past governors had done. Rather, he had every intention of doing just that. Governor Christie wasn't bluffing. One might ask, why was the governor telling me about his intentions? The primary reason was that I headed up a non-profit, independent production company called the Caucus Educational Corporation (CEC) established in 1994 with strong ties to the PBS flagship station in New York, WNET. Our organization was and is very entrepreneurial, and we didn't receive any direct state government subsidy. All of our funding comes from corporate, foundation and individual sources. Further, we provided a significant amount of programming for our public broadcasting partners. WNET was and is a major PBS station in New York with a well-earned reputation for producing and broadcasting excellent educational, cultural, and public affairs programming.

Leading Change Requires a Strong Quarterback

To his credit, WNET Group President and CEO Neal Shapiro, who was formerly the head of NBC News, was and is a tremendous leader who is innovative in his thinking and clearly understood the changing nature of broadcast media. Neal was ahead of the curve at the time and thinking more and more about innovative and creative different ways of producing and distributing content on digital platforms. As a leader at WNET Group, Neal Shapiro understood that a traditional audience for broadcast television was becoming fragmented and shrinking as people consumed information in a variety of alternative ways that have now become the norm. Neal and his team also understood the need to run a tight ship to produce quality programming with fewer resources and people and, like the CEC, they were really good at fundraising.

Some of the folks at NJN aggressively fought Governor Chris Christie's effort to eliminate state funding to their station. Except, as Governor of New Jersey, Chris Christie had the ability to eliminate that $11 million plus in state funding to NJN by simply using a "red pen" and taking these line items out of the state budget. If and when he did that, the real question became how would New Jersey's public broadcasting network pivot—adapt—and innovate in the ways needed to create a new model of a more scaled down, efficient, but highly entrepreneurial network, no longer staying alive with a huge, annual state subsidy? That was the stark reality in 2010. That was the climate and the environment around all of us connected to public broadcasting. It was a fact of life as leaders—we would either embrace it or stick our heads in the sand and hope for the best. As I've said in my previous books for leaders who are facing daunting challenges and obstacles, "hope is not a plan."

Yet, the CWA leadership, representing over 130 public employees at NJN, refused to see the graphic writing on the wall. But if NJN's leadership was not going to take the initiative with the required sense of urgency to create a different organizational model outside of state government, then who could and would? Enter WNET and its leader Neal Shapiro. To his credit, Shapiro did not want to see public broadcasting go away in New Jersey. But it would be daunting and challenging to create a new network from scratch—especially in a very short period of time. To take on that responsibility and financial burden (full disclosure, with the cooperation of the CEC and other independent programmers), WNET decided to put their hat in the ring in a bid to take over public broadcasting in New Jersey, assuming that NJN would in fact be eliminated.

To be clear, Governor Christie needed legislative approval to allow WNET, or any other private, non-government agency, to take over public broadcasting. The proposed name of a potential new network in New Jersey was NJTV. However, if the state legislature voted to reject the WNET bid to create a new, more independent broadcasting model, that station on the TV dial would have gone "dark," a black hole that would cause New Jersey to have no PBS station, which would make it the only one of 50 states in our country with such an embarrassing reality. Neal Shapiro had made it clear that as a leader in the public media universe— he didn't want to see that happen.

Many at NJN and the CWA fought this inevitable change with all of their might. They accused WNET of being a New York-centric network that would be an interloper in New Jersey, this despite the fact that WNET committed publicly to producing and broadcasting over 20 hours of "New Jersey-centric" content—some of which would be produced by our not-for-profit Caucus Educational Corporation. Some of those folks accused me and the CEC of having nefarious and selfish motives, in which NJTV would somehow push a "political agenda" that would benefit Governor Christie and somehow other political players that were never mentioned by name. They said that Governor Christie was "giving" a New Jersey network away, ignoring the fact that if approved, WNET would be responsible for the new network and that once again, the challenge of raising millions of dollars to create and sustain such an operation. This was something few if any other private organizations had the willingness or ability to accomplish.

Some at NJN and CWA testified before the state legislature, wrote opinion pieces fighting the NJTV plan. They also said this "change" would cause 130 NJN employees to lose their jobs. They said this was Governor Chris Christie engaged in "union busting." Their attacks were relentless. Yet, in my view, they offered no plan themselves, no real leadership, no ability to adapt, pivot or change themselves. All they would say was that any new effort was wrong and unnecessary.

There were "offline" conversations that took place with NJN leaders, some of whom were on air personalities who were fighting WNET's effort to save public broadcasting in New Jersey. In some of those conversations, the folks at NJN kept saying their plan was to "stop NJTV." Many of us aligned with WNET tried to say basically this; "Look, change is inevitable. If NJTV didn't become New Jersey's new PBS station, then there would be no public broadcasting in our state with over 9 million people."

Also consider that NJTV, if approved, would be a potential place for some of NJN's most talented professionals. And to be clear, there were many excellent team members at NJN. No deal. The CWA's unofficial position was that either all of its 130 employees would keep their jobs, or they would try to stop NJTV's creation. As I said, simply put, they were insisting on maintaining the status quo as if the status quo were actually an option, knowing that Governor Christie was in fact eliminating well over $11 million of a state subsidy to NJN—with the clock ticking very quickly. Without that state subsidy, NJN would die and, in turn, no one at the network would have a job.

In the end, New Jersey's State Senate voted to approve the WNET proposal to create NJTV. The challenge, as I said, of creating a new, innovative, and highly entrepreneurial PBS network led by WNET Group President and CEO Neal Shapiro was daunting. This would take great leadership, tremendous innovation, and adaptability and yes, a sense of urgency. The irony is that as soon as NJTV became official, many of the employees at NJN wanted to be a part of it. To his credit, Neal Shapiro and his NJTV colleagues recruited some of NJN's talented professionals to be a part of the new network. NJTV was officially launched on July 1, 2011, with a small but dedicated team.

A decade later, NJTV was renamed NJ PBS and today is a thriving and respected media organization that produces a first-rate nightly news program called NJ Spotlight News—produced in cooperation with NJ Spotlight, a quality media news organization, which joined the WNET Group. Clearly Shapiro and his team embraced the idea of creating news and public affairs content in a more innovative fashion and distributing it on multiple digital platforms. NJ PBS provides quality, impactful programming to over 9 million people in the Garden State and I am proud to say that some of that programming is produced by the Caucus

Educational Corporation as one of the many independent organizations providing programming content for NJ PBS. Again, the CEC doesn't receive a penny in a direct state subsidy. We are responsible for raising all of the money needed to produce and distribute our content. NJ PBS has a similar entrepreneurial culture with a strong development and fundraising team.

Either You Lead the Change or Change Will Happen to You

Readers may wonder why I have chosen to share this detailed saga about public broadcasting. Here's why. As the title of this chapter says; "Change, Innovate, Adapt or Die." Some of the professionals at NJN, a respected public broadcasting network for 41 years (along with the CWA) either couldn't or wouldn't adapt or innovate. They didn't change while the media universe was going through a dramatic paradigm shift. They clung to the status quo as if it were a realistic and viable option in the face of Governor Chris Christie telling anyone who would listen that he was going to eliminate the network and slash well over $11 million in an annual state subsidy from the state budget. That was an inevitable and painful fact of life. That wasn't going to change. The only thing that could change was how those most impacted chose to respond.

I genuinely feel for the people at NJN who lost their jobs with the elimination of their network, No decent person wants to see people lose their livelihood. But great leadership sometimes involves taking bold and decisive action for the larger good. That's what WNET tried to do with the creation of NJTV, now NJ PBS. When industries evolve—when the world and circumstances and forces around you change—organizations and their leaders must change, innovate, adapt accordingly or they often can't survive. The case of NJN is obviously not the only one in which an organization couldn't adapt strategically, operationally and financially to a rapidly changing landscape. But it is a case study that I am intimately, professionally, and personally aware of and experienced first-hand. The case reinforced for me as a student of leadership what the price of resisting change can be even for a respected organization and how innovative, creative and bold leadership is the only realistic option in these very challenging, uncertain, and ever-changing times.

I will always appreciate WNET Group President and CEO Neal Shapiro's leadership and willingness to take on the challenge, along with his colleagues, to help save public broadcasting in New Jersey. When you think about the case of NJN in this context, consider that many organizations, companies, and industries that couldn't or wouldn't adapt or evolve to stay competitive and thriving. Here is just a short list; Blockbuster. Kodak®. Most newspapers. Blackberry. Xerox®. MySpace. Sears. RadioShack. Clearly, such a list is always changing.

The Only Constant is Change

As I've often stated in my leadership seminars; "Clearly, I don't make the rules, but I am confident I know what they are..." One of those rules is that while we would all like in certain cases for things to simply "stay the same", that's just not possible. A very smart person once said, "The only constant is change." So true. There is no debating this.

So be innovative, agile, adaptable, flexible, and bold. Be the kind of strategic leader that "connects the dots," makes the necessary pivot and adjustment to stay in the game. Being innovative it is not an option or simply a desirable leadership trait, it is an absolute necessity. If COVID hasn't reinforced this reality, I can't imagine what will. More than 2 years of a global pandemic isn't simply about Zoom, it is about the need to constantly be thinking about new and creative ways to lead your organization in these very uncertain and sobering times. So here is the bottom line—like it or not; "change, innovate, adapt or die." Like I said, as leaders, we may not be able to control the ever-changing forces in our universe, but we have a lot of control over how we choose to respond. Change, innovate and adapt...The alternative isn't an option for those of us who call ourselves leaders.

Chapter 3
The Best Leaders "Own It"...Quickly

I'm fascinated by the critical question of "taking responsibility" or as I've come to describe it as "owning it!" As leaders—even the best leaders—we make lots of mistakes. We do things we regret. We screw up. We make boneheaded decisions. I wonder why? Obviously, it's because we're human beings. "Perfect" leaders just don't exist because perfection is an illusion—not to mention the definition of perfection is highly subjective. Let's be clear, I find myself "owning" a lot of things I've done wrong, both in my professional and personal life. In fact, I've apologized so often that Mary and my wife Jen have questions as to whether sometimes I use the term, "I own it," as a way to get out of the conversation and a less than preferable situation a lot sooner.

NO EXCUSES...

Okay...I have to "own" that there is some truth to what Mary and Jen say, but of my many leadership faults, quickly admitting that I'm wrong and "owning it" (and working not to repeat the same mistake or behavior) is something I'm proud of. To try to keep myself consistent (not perfect but hopefully improving) in this critical area of leadership, I have a very large framed poster in our home gym that says "NO EXCUSES." It's my way of reminding myself that most of our "excuses" are pretty lame. Of course, we all make excuses. I know I do. (Especially when it comes to late night snacking as well as my less-than-constructive responses as a leader when things go wrong, or mistakes are made on our team.) But here's the deal when it comes to leadership; in the majority of cases, nobody cares about your "excuses." I'm not talking about a leader's serious health issue or a major family or personal issue. I'm talking about the "dog ate my homework" stuff. Ask yourself, what is the price we—and our organization pay for making these excuses, rather than owning our mistakes?

Owning ALL of It Isn't Easy

Being a great leader is not easy. Sometimes it doesn't even seem fair that you as the leader are responsible for everything that happens within your "universe." That's crazy, right? As CEO and the executive producer of the Caucus Educational Corporation, I don't operate the cameras. I don't put the fonts on the TV screen. I don't run the audio board. I didn't write every e-mail to every sponsor or program and produce every segment. I don't even write every grant proposal or pitch to a sponsor (Mary leads that effort). And to be clear, while I love marketing and promotion, I don't design all of our promotional ads or social media posts about our programming. At Stand & Deliver, our leadership and communications firm, I don't manage the seminar and executive coaching schedule. I don't produce and edit every "Lessons in Leadership" podcast where Mary serves as executive producer. I don't compile our seminar materials. And no, I am not the editor of this book.

But as the leader of both the Caucus Educational Corporation and Stand & Deliver, and author of this book, I have to be responsible for all of it. Everything, including the quality of every on-camera interview that is ever aired and produced by both organizations. Think about that. Even if a specific team member makes the mistake or falls short on his or her performance, I either hired that person directly or hired the person who hired that person. I either coached that team member or put someone in a position to coach or mentor that team member. You get it? The kind of great leadership that I'm talking about is an extremely high standard. It's often not easy, and at times it doesn't seem fair. But the best leaders have only one choice and that is to own it—all of it. Whatever goes wrong, whatever mistakes are made, to our key stakeholders, be it a sponsor, a guest on a program, a Stand & Deliver client, a media partner, etc., there is only one response that I or any leader can have and it sounds like this; "What happened is not okay. It is on me. I take full responsibility for this situation. Let me talk to our team and get back to you with how we can make this right. I assure you I will do all I need to do as our team leader to make sure this doesn't happen again."

To be clear, a leader's job is challenging in that regard. A very candid and real conversation needs to take place within the team about what went wrong, why it happened, who "owns" it internally and what exactly must be done (by when and by whom) to do all that can be done to make sure the "mistake" is not repeated.

The Case of Zach Wilson

What really strikes me is how difficult it is for so many in positions of leadership to take responsibility for their poor performance or that of the team they lead. I am writing this chapter during the 2022 NFL season. As you can tell from reading this book, I really like sports. I play a few, but mainly I watch. I was watching the NY Jets on a recent Sunday as their second-year, 23-year-old highly-paid first round draft choice quarterback Zach Wilson had played the worst game I have ever seen someone play as quarterback. The quarterback on most football teams is considered a team leader. In fact, Wilson was named team captain of the Jets by team management to signify his leadership position. They put a big, bold C on his jersey to make it official. But it wasn't Wilson's poor play as quarterback that makes this case study worthy of examining. It was his pitiful post-game press conference in which he was asked if he felt his dreadful performance let the Jets defense, who played a nearly flawless game, down. His very curt and reflex response was, "NO!" Ouch.

Wilson went on to say his poor passing performance (A total of 2-yards in the second half) was a product of the "wind" during the game, even though the opposing quarterback through for nearly 300 yards during the game. Talk about excuses. Why is it that the Zach Wilson case study is less about football and more about leadership? I say it is simple. We all play bad games and have bad days. It happens even to the best in their respective field. But as soon as Zach Wilson refused or was incapable to simply say in response to a predictable question (See chapter "Don't Sweat the Q&A") about letting the Jets defense down and saying, "No" the internet exploded.

The next day sports commentators, including many ex-quarterbacks, blasted Wilson's lack of leadership. He was trashed for not taking responsibility for his poor performance. He was trashed even more for his post-game press conference. He was described as not having the maturity to understand that being the quarterback—having that big fat C on his jersey—meant that he was the team leader who simply could have said—even before the first predictable media question after such a terrible game; "Let me simply say that I played poorly. There is no excuse. We all played in the same conditions and I just didn't play well enough, especially given how terrific our defense played. I have to get better and I am going to work extra hard to make sure my play improves for our next game."

If Zach Wilson had said anything remotely like this (he should have been prepped and coached by the Jets' communication team to handle the post-game press conference) he could have avoided the very negative fallback that included being benched for the next game and replaced by his backup quarterback, as well as the apparent resentment he faced from many teammates who were angry and disappointed in Wilson's refusal to "own" his terrible performance. To be clear, the silver lining here is that the Zach Wilson story has a postscript. A couple of days after that press conference, Wilson, again only 23, shared that his father reached out for him and told him how bad he looked in the post-game press conference. He asked his son if he understood the impact of him not taking any responsibility for the outcome of the game and responding "no" to whether he let down the team's defense. Zach Wilson responded that he wasn't even thinking clearly and responded in kneejerk fashion. He then apologized, but unfortunately, too much damage was done at that point. Too much time had passed, and this leadership opportunity was missed.

Joe Biden and Donald Trump: Owning It?

You see, Wilson's initial refusal or inability to own his significant role in a team defeat is quite common for leaders in every arena. We see it in board rooms and C-suites. We see it with university presidents and our elected officials at the highest level. As I have stated very clearly in this book, Donald Trump's refusal to simply own that he lost the 2020 election or own his part in the tragedy of the January 6 insurrection (for meeting with known anti-semites and white supremacists) speaks for itself. And President Joe Biden—while having very different political views than Donald Trump—seems to share the affliction of refusing or being unable to "own" very public failures and/or mistakes around the withdrawal of troops in Afghanistan as well as acknowledging that inflation and the economy have been exacerbated under his watch. (Ironically both Trump and Biden refused to "own" their sloppy handling of classified documents that should have never wound up either at Mar-a-Lago or in Biden's garage in Delaware next to his beloved Corvette.)

As for Biden, it's not that he's solely to blame or responsible for inflation, but most leaders, including Presidents of the United States, are more than eager to take *credit* when the economy is strong and the stock market is soaring, but seem to have a real problem accepting any responsibility or owning any part of an economic downturn. The point is, it happened on your watch and in your universe, so as leaders our job is to share the credit when things are going well and own our part exclusively when things go wrong.

In my book *What Were They Thinking* published in 2008, I outlined numerous examples—primarily in the world of business—of leaders simply not taking responsibility for a very public mistake, no matter how big or how small. And in the book, *Extreme Ownership* written by Navy Seals Jocko Willink and Leif Babin, the authors describe their view on how military and other leaders must take full responsibility for everything and anything that goes wrong on their watch—even if the mistake or mishap took place at the hands of an individual team member or members.

Hank Keirsey Owned It and Paid the Price

A powerful example of this extreme ownership approach to leadership was described in my book, *Lessons in Leadership,* where Hank Keirsey, a high-ranking military official, had the misfortune of having one of the members of his platoon insert a pornographic slide in a PowerPoint presentation that was never intended to be made public. When the PowerPoint did go public, it was a tremendous embarrassment for the military. While Hank Keirsey didn't create and insert the slide itself, he took full responsibility for the mishap. Unfortunately, a military trial ensued and Keirsey not only lost his rank but was dismissed from the military. Think about that. When I've shared the Hank Keirsey story in our leadership seminars, some praised Keirsey as a brave leader with a high level of accountability and integrity. Others, however, questioned Keirsey's judgment with one seminar participant recently saying; "But he lost his job. His career ended. How does that help anyone?" That's a legitimate point of view, but the moral is clear. We don't own or accept responsibility when we are confident that there will be no consequences for us, professionally and/or personally. We own and accept responsibility for bad outcomes because that is extraordinary leadership that most of us are either incapable or unwilling to execute.

Colin Powell Made Mistakes and Owned Them All

In the original *Lessons in Leadership* book, I wrote a chapter featuring the exceptional leadership traits of the late General Colin Powell. The chapter is called "Great Leaders Sometimes Piss People Off." That pithy quote came directly from an interview I did with the late General Powell in 1998 in which I asked him about the keys to great leadership. What struck me is that he said that the best leaders must make tough decisions, including ones that will not be popular with certain team members or key stakeholders, because the leader believes that particular decision is best for the team or organization. General Powell argued that many leaders are either unable or unwilling to make those difficult decisions, whether in the military or in any type of organization.

But it is also General Powell's integrity and character as a leader that for me makes him a role model for so many of us who study and try to emulate his leadership approach. I'm sure some reading this will say, "But what about his role in the US Iraqi War?" I get it, but, consider that publicly and unequivocally he took responsibility for the failure of his February 2003 United Nations' testimony in which he emphatically claimed that Iraq and Saddam Hussein possessed "weapons of mass destruction" – which was largely the justification for the United States going to war at the time. General Powell trusted a variety of government intelligence and military agencies and their conclusions which, ultimately, were proven to be false. They were simply wrong. There were no weapons of mass destruction that were ever found. In turn, the premise of the U.S. going to war in Iraq was faulty and illegitimate.

Clearly, this intelligence information and subsequent conclusions needed to be challenged more aggressively in this critical juncture in US and Iraqi relations—post 9/11.

But while so many leaders – particularly in public life – point fingers, make excuses, scapegoat, and deflect, that is not what General Powell did. In fact, he stood up and said HE was wrong, and HE was responsible for accepting those intelligence reports without questioning or challenging them more aggressively. He trusted but acknowledged that he did not verify to the degree he should have. In spite of this, he pointed no fingers and blamed no one else. Yes, General Powell explained how the intelligence process played out leading to his UN testimony. Ultimately, he took the hit—in a very public way. Just think about how rare that is for leaders of any stripe. According to General Powell from an NBC interview on "Meet the Press" from September 2015, "If we had known the intelligence was wrong, we would not have gone into Iraq. But the intelligence community, all 16 agencies, assured us that it was right." Further, while so many leaders often say they have "no regrets" in their careers, Powell said of his most important UN testimony, "I will always regret it."

Some have argued that General Powell "lied" in his UN testimony regarding Iraqi "Weapons of Mass Destruction." I understand this thinking especially given the death of so many Iraqis and US soldiers involved in the US war in Iraq. The war was tragic and clearly based on flawed intelligence and the potentially misguided motives of some in the Bush White House. However, I don't believe that Colin Powell "lied" in his UN testimony, but rather made a series of serious and deadly mistakes for which he not only apologized and regretted, but he acknowledged the terrible impact of these mistakes. Yet, mistakes, no matter how serious, do not equate to leaders who "lie" or intentionally deceive (consider disgraced former New York Governor Andrew Cuomo and his administration at the height of the COVID pandemic intentionally undercounting by nearly half the number of deaths that took place in New York State nursing homes. This was after Cuomo's fateful decision to send nursing home patients who were treated in hospitals back into their nursing homes without ensuring that those around them, including other patients and staff, would be protected. Is that lying? Is it not deceptive? By any reasonable standard, this was a governmental decision and not simply a "mistake.")

The issue involving Governor Cuomo, as well as his counterpart in New Jersey, Governor Phil Murphy, who made the same decision to send COVID treated nursing home patients back into unprotected nursing home facilities, and in turn, refused to simply acknowledge that a serious mistake was made. I've interviewed Governor Murphy regarding this topic on several occasions and every time he has pushed back, arguing that he did nothing wrong in this regard and has no regrets.

Conversely, General Colin Powell didn't lie about Iraq's "Weapons of Mass Destruction," nor did he intentionally deceive his International UN audience. Leaders—even the best leaders—make big mistakes—mistakes that have tragic consequences, particularly when the stakes are so high. The reason is as simple as it is complex, but it revolves around the fact that we are all flawed, imperfect people who do and say things that we regret or at least should regret. I've never understood leaders or any individual saying that they have, "no regrets" about any aspect of the decisions they've made in their life.

So, while we remember General Powell for his many accomplishments, what I admire most about him is that he was the kind of leader who took full responsibility for his actions, words, and mistakes. This type of leader shouldn't be so rare, but obviously is. So, thank you, General Powell, for all you did for our country and the standard you set for all leaders who must do better and be better, particularly those leaders in public service who have falsely concluded that taking responsibility or admitting one's own mistakes is somehow a sign of weakness, which couldn't be further from the truth. The late General Colin Powell—flawed and imperfect like all of us—left a powerful legacy of leadership and integrity for all of us to follow.

Chapter 4
Feedback is a Funny Thing:
"Just Don't Be Yourself, Dad"

In my last book *Lessons in Leadership*, I talked extensively about feedback in a chapter called "Receiving Feedback: Can You Handle the Truth?" Over the past several years, I have been thinking a lot more about why receiving and giving feedback is so challenging for so many leaders. Feedback is complex, but it is essential to developing ourselves as leaders and as individuals, as well as helping to develop those around us.

In my leadership seminar series, Mary and I ask each participant to conduct what we call a "mini-360 feedback exercise," where they ask several colleagues, including those they report to, those they work with as well as those who report to them, two key questions. The first question is, "What are my two greatest leadership strengths?" It is great to have this positive feedback that tells you how good you are in certain areas. But this exercise becomes more challenging when you get to the second question, which is to ask those around you to identify two, possibly three "opportunities to improve as a leader" and provide specific examples for each.

Every leader who wants to be his or her best proactively seeks and needs candid and constructive feedback. It sounds obvious, I know. But as they say, "easier said than done!" No matter how evolved we think we are as leaders or how high our emotional intelligence quotient is, real feedback that talks about your "opportunities to improve" is not natural or easy for most of us to hear as well as to offer such feedback to colleagues.

Most of us are initially defensive. Our instincts kick in and we tend to disagree, deflect and defend and we explain that the feedback giver "just doesn't understand." I know this because I have reacted in this fashion on countless occasions, which is why a bit of self-disclosure will help better explain why for me feedback has been such a funny thing. (And I don't mean ha-ha funny.)

Other than my mother, who usually tells me what a great son I am (and rarely, if ever, gives me constructive or critical feedback) the 3 women I am closest to are my wife of 20+ years, Jennifer, our 11-year-old daughter, Olivia, and yes, Mary Gamba, my colleague and work partner of 21+ years. Each of these 3 strong women consistently give me feedback—often the kind of feedback that I don't particularly like hearing—or end up resisting. Again, I am not talking about praise or recognition, the kind of feedback anyone would love to hear. I am talking about the tough stuff, the opportunities to improve in areas that are blind spots for us as leaders and individuals. Here are a few examples.

I have written about how Mary has confronted me in the past on my tendency to "blame first" and "overreact" to things that go wrong in our organization. I know I am a pretty strong, strategic (connecting the dots) leader who is good at solving certain problems, but it is how I get there that at times has been problematic. Overreacting to a mistake by not initially managing my emotions has caused me to lash out and be hypercritical of certain individuals. (I would say that was the "old Steve" vs. a "new" more evolved Steve. But Mary will share her thoughts on this.) For years I would ask Mary, "Who exactly screwed up?" But as Mary has told me, perseverating on who screwed up often gets in the way of moving to "solution mode." Further, by the time we actually got to a solution or resolution, Mary has offered feedback to me making it clear that there was often unnecessary roadkill along the way, which potentially de-motivated team members or the team overall. For the longest time I would argue with Mary that I was just holding our team to a higher standard of excellence. That may have been true, but again, it is how I would attempt to get there as a leader that would often fall short and create unnecessary problems.

Over time, I came to realize that I needed to adjust my overall approach and mindset about things going wrong and retrain my leadership "muscle memory" to better understand what had gone wrong and quickly move to exploring potential solutions or remedies without simply focusing on "who screwed up!" It should never have taken this many years and so many unnecessary arguments and debates with Mary to get to this point, however, as I said, "feedback is a funny thing." On some level, the critical feedback felt personal and, therefore, I felt the need to explain and defend for many years before I was open to change and trying to understand.

"Quickly move to solution mode when things go wrong"

According to Mary, the feedback was never personal, and after more than two-decades of working together, she consistently reminds me of how far we have come. Says Mary, "Working for the 'old Steve' when things didn't go as planned was often draining, exhausting, and frustrating, and made me question my own self-worth. However, I took a risk and provided very specific feedback to Steve on where he needed to improve. To his credit, he now quickly moves to 'solution mode' when things go wrong, and our professional relationship, and the overall morale of the team, has improved tremendously as a result."

As for my wife, Jennifer, several years ago I asked her how I could be a "better husband and father" to our 3 children. At the time, both of our boys, Nick and Chris, were heavily involved in sports and our daughter Olivia who was starting kindergarten, was getting involved in soccer, gymnastics, etc. Many of our kids' activities were on the weekends, which presented some challenges for me.

My wife's very specific, "constructive feedback" went like this; "I notice you play golf on both Saturday and Sunday. Do you really need to play both days, because when you do, you miss a lot of the kids' games?" She was absolutely right, but here is how I initially responded; "Jen, you are kidding me, right? I make a lot of the kids' games, plus, I work my ass off all week and one of the few outlets from work I have is playing golf on the weekends. I play early in the morning so I can be finished before noon. Some other guys play golf in the afternoon and hang out at the golf course smoking cigars and drinking for the rest of the day." Clearly frustrated, Jennifer responded that many of our kids' activities are in the morning, which created a scheduling conflict. She suggested I play only one day each weekend, but pathetically, I continued to defend myself. In fact, Jennifer got in the habit of calling me "Single Steve Saturday" or

"Single Steve Sunday" to tease me when I would check out and do my own thing on a weekend day. I basically argued with Jen that my hard work and business success allowed us as a family to have a great quality life and that I shouldn't be criticized for how I spend the weekends. This of course made no sense because we had 3 kids who needed my attention, and I was simply too selfish with my "free time" to appreciate it. Not to mention I wasn't being the father and husband I wanted to be.

Finally, my wife said to me, "Why did you ask how you could be a better father and husband if you didn't want me to give you an answer?" So, there it was. You can't argue with feedback because when you ask someone you respect and care about for their perception of how you can "improve," that is exactly what you are going to get. You can't argue that they don't see it that way, nor can you simply explain away or defend your actions, which doesn't change that person's perception of you. It's counterproductive and often leads to stupid arguments and unhealthy communication.

Over time, I have adjusted my schedule and became much more engaged and involved in our children's activities. My golf game is no better or worse for it. Additionally, once Jennifer saw that I finally responded to her feedback she offered more of it like, "You know that recycling is on Mondays and garbage on Tuesday and Friday, and I noticed that you seem to forget that." The only problem is that now, every time I take out the garbage or recycling, I am looking for a gold medal, which isn't the point, is it? LOL.

Finally, as for our daughter Olivia, who as I said is strong-willed, confident and not afraid to tell me what she thinks, here is a vivid example. On her first day of middle school, I of course wanted to drive her, so along with my wife, we are on our way to the school and as we pull up, our daughter asked us to let her out a bit away from the front of the building. My response was, "Olivia, can't I walk with you on your first day?" She said, "Dad, I'm almost 11. You don't need to walk me." As she walked away from the car, I opened the window and said loudly, "Olivia, dad loves you. Hope you have a great day. Are you sure I can't walk with you?" Apparently embarrassed in front of the other kids, Olivia just blurted out, "Dad, just don't be yourself." To which my wife responded, "Yeah, stop being Steve Adubato." Ouch, that hurt.

But what they meant was that I was potentially making a scene in public as Olivia walked into her new school. She was embarrassed and didn't want her dad drawing attention to her. She was right, but of course I was a bit hurt and felt crappy. But the more I thought about it, I realized she was giving me constructive feedback that I needed to listen to. I didn't want to hear it, because I would rather have our daughter say, "Dad you are the best. Give me a big hug and hold my hand because it is my first day." But that is more about me and my needs, and not what a soon to be 11-year-old needed.

Simply put, this whole feedback thing is something that has confounded me for years. You can write about it, teach and coach people to be receptive to feedback, but until you step back and really think about your own reaction to constructive / critical feedback, you can't appreciate how difficult that can be. But the irony is that the only way for any of us to improve or grow in any area as leaders, fathers, husbands, etc., is to seek and be open to such hard to hear feedback. We have to fight the urge to resist, defend or over-explain our actions.

Some of my clients have pushed back and said, "That's fine, but what if I disagree with the feedback?" My response is always the same. You can disagree and even ignore it, but you can't argue with the feedback of someone you trust and respect because, as I said, that is how they view you and your actions. The only problem with ignoring the feedback is it sends the message to the feedback giver that you don't care that much and their opinion isn't of any great value. Further, it has the potential to hurt that relationship and finally, if you do choose to ignore feedback because you disagree with it, you miss an opportunity to improve. Think about it. What exactly do we have to lose by accepting critical feedback as the gift that it is and choose to do something about it? To work on that area as an opportunity to grow and get better?

Finally, let's return to the 360-feedback exercise. Some of the opportunities to improve identified by our clients involve being more concise, better managing our time, having more confidence when communicating in public, being more open to others' points of view, the need to be a better listener and to be more present, etc. Mary and I have seen so many of the people we work with grow and improve and ultimately accept at least a portion of this critical feedback and decide to do something about it. These are leaders who over time become stronger public presenters and better coaches and mentors, as well as more present and active listeners. Our leadership development clients who grow and improve in this way say that it is extremely rewarding.

One caveat with the 360-mini feedback exercise is that numerous professionals we have coached over the years insist that those they ask for constructive feedback around "opportunities to improve" say they just can't think of anything. That's ridiculous. In fact, Mary and I tell our clients to insist that those they trust and respect give them at least one area or opportunity to improve. Further, we tell them if they get no initial response, to push harder because "no one is perfect." However, I would be less than honest to say that we have succeeded in every case because it takes a degree of persistence on the part of the leader asking for the feedback as well as a trusting relationship that is based on mutual respect. The resistance to giving constructive feedback is often just as confounding and problematic as the resistance and defensiveness to hearing and receiving it. Another reason why feedback is such a funny thing.

Here is a constructive way to assertively encourage meaningful, constructive feedback, from a reluctant colleague on how you can improve. Simply say; "Jim, your opinion matters to me. I really want to improve as a leader and your feedback is going to help me do just that. Tell me one area where I can improve. That doesn't mean I am terrible, it is just that I can get better and stronger when it comes to XYZ. If I can't get that feedback, it is going to be hard for me to get better."

So, here is the deal. The next time you either ask for constructive feedback from someone you respect and care about, or he or she offers it without you even asking, choose to be open. Choose to not be defensive. Choose to do something about it. You not only have nothing to lose, but you have everything to gain. For all of us, instead of trying to "make our case" as to why we are the way we are or do what we do or don't do, consider that none of us are perfect, nor is that the goal. Great leadership is all about progress, not perfection. Rather, our goal is constant improvement and the only way that happens is by seeing feedback as the gift that it is and openly accepting and embracing it.

Chapter 5
It's a Question of Confidence

Let's talk leadership and confidence. According to successful entrepreneur Francisco Dao; "Self-confidence is the fundamental basis from which leadership grows. Trying to teach leadership without first building confidence is like building a house on a foundation of sand. It may have a nice coat of paint, but it is ultimately shaky at best."

I've been coaching and teaching about leadership for well over two decades, focusing on such topics as; effective presentations, leading and facilitating engaging meetings, artfully but directly confronting difficult issues and circumstances, accepting and receiving feedback, as well as a variety of other leadership-related matters. Yet, I realized in preparing to write this book, and in the process of selecting the chapters for it, I have never actually written about confidence and its connection to great leadership. I'm not sure why that's the case, except to conclude that I frankly haven't really felt very confident to do so. Ironic, I get it. Fact is, there are many times in my life as a leadership coach, author, and leader of organizations, as well as a father, husband, friend (and long-time avid golfer) that I have felt less than confident. I think I thought the only way to write about confidence is to feel confident in virtually every situation or circumstance you face. Of course, you begin to realize that this notion is absurd. Nobody is confident 100% or even 99% of the time. In fact, when people say they are that supremely confident (in every situation or circumstance), I am a bit skeptical.

Confidence is Not a Constant

Think about it. Even the best of the best has their confidence tested and shaken at times. I've seen Steph Curry, one of the greatest pure shooters in NBA history and possibly the best, most consistent foul shooter, miss 3 or 4 free throws in a row in a tightly contested playoff game. Is that solely a question of skill? I doubt it. Could that have anything to do with confidence? As a NY Yankee fan, I've seen one of the most dominant relief pitchers, Aroldis Chapman (who had a history of throwing 100-miles-per-hour or more) striking out opposing players in a dominant fashion and then staring them down. Months later, and in the process of coming back after being injured and rehabbing, the same supremely confident pitcher lost the strike zone and walked multiple players in a row. Chapman simply couldn't find the strike zone after being uber-confident for many years. One more Yankee example. Aaron Judge, who hit 62 home runs in 2022 and was the MVP in the American League, had one of the most successful seasons a player could have. However, in the playoffs, Aaron Judge didn't perform well at all. He struck out a lot and his power as a hitter seemed to have been lost. Was that all a question of execution? Or, did Aaron Judge's lack of confidence in the more high-pressured playoffs have anything to do with his struggles?

Yet, it's not just how fleeting, or at times confounding, confidence is in sports. This phenomenon is just as real in every arena or profession, including when it comes to leadership. Let me clarify how I view confidence. I'm not talking about a leader who communicates with bluster, arrogance and defensiveness and believes that he or she is always right, refusing to admit his or her mistakes while blaming others in the process (think President's Donald Trump and Joe Biden on too many occasions when things have gone wrong on their leadership watch). To me, that "leadership" is simply about hubris, along with a lack of humility or self-awareness. That's not confidence in my book. I've come to see confidence not as a black and white thing, but rather something that ebbs and flows—even with the best in their respective field. It's not that confidence is like a light switch that goes on and off, but there are degrees of it in certain situations that in my view is based largely on how a leader (or any person) chooses to see themselves in a particular situation. I also know that confidence is a product of consistent success and receiving positive feedback, which only adds to your confidence level. Yet, I am more intrigued by how we as leaders can put ourselves in a "more confident frame of mind," without the benefit of recent success along with praise and recognition from others. How can we as leaders view virtually any situation or challenge as an opportunity to confidently deal with it and be at our best, knowing that mistakes and mishaps are just part of the process? Perhaps as good leaders we are able to do just that because we have resilience (and grit), and we don't let mistakes prevent us from moving forward. We are aware of the past and our leadership shortcomings, and rather than obsess over them (or ignore them) we must always learn from them and grow.

My Confidence is a Mixed Bag

Some personal disclosure may be helpful, as I share just a bit of my experience with the issue of confidence. My wife recently told me, as I told her that I was writing this chapter, that she saw me as a "very confident person." In fact, some leadership seminar participants and friends have even told me that my confidence can actually border on cockiness. Fact is, my confidence level at best is a very mixed bag. There have been times in my life that I have had great confidence, when I've been convinced that I had what it took to not only succeed, but to succeed in a big way. Confidence that I was in the zone—on my game—doing what I do well and making a positive impact with the odds of success being pretty high. It could be leading a seminar, keynote speech, coaching a client, on the air on public broadcasting conducting an interview or providing commentary on an important topic or issue on a local or national media platform.

At times, I've even felt confident in my golf game. A six-foot putt to win a match ("I've got this.") A delicate chip shot from 70 years away. I can clearly see the shot in my mind with a 60-degree wedge as I tell myself; "You are going to put this on the pin." Then, when COVID hit in early 2020, and while fearful, like most of us, I felt confident I would work with other team members, particularly my colleague Mary Gamba, to keep our organization on track, pivot, adapt and in fact get even stronger in the process.

Yet, here is the opposite side of the confidence coin from my perspective. I distinctly remember losing my seat in the NJ State Legislature in the mid-1980s. During the campaign, at only 27-years-of-age, I worked with a dedicated team of volunteers and staff in my re-election effort to try to win that race. But when I lost by a narrow margin, I was defeated, dejected, and lost, and my confidence level was at a long time low. I remember saying things to myself like, "Why me? How could I lose? This was my professional dream to get elected to the state legislature and then run for Congress in a couple of years. And then become the youngest governor or US Senator in NJ history." Now what? I was confident of all this until those sobering election results in 1985, in which the voters in my district suggested that I change my career plans. That is when the deep sense of self-doubt crept in; "*What if* I'm seen as a loser whose political career was a flash in a pan? Two years and done! *What if* I am no longer the young man on the rise on the political scene and lose my momentum?" I had zero confidence at the time. I was feeling sorry for myself, and I know I was not a lot of fun to be around. P.S. It didn't help that my father, the late Steve Adubato, Sr, said at the time; "Okay—you lost—so you are a loser. Now stop feeling sorry for yourself and come to work for me and my organization!" Thanks, dad. LOL.

Mentors Matter in the Confidence Game

But I got lucky and that is a funny thing about leadership and life. Sometimes we just get lucky. At 27 years-old, and now a lame duck state legislator about to leave office, I had an older and wiser mentor named Jerry Grecco, who has since passed away. Jerry was my campaign chairman when I ran for the NJ State Legislature at 25 and unexpectantly won two years earlier. I remember Jerry taking me to lunch a couple of weeks after that losing that election and telling me what I needed to hear; "Look, you are a very young man. Okay, you've lost. But look what you accomplished. You raised a lot of money, built a strong team and you have a solid reputation, and you are pretty good communicator. This is an opportunity for you." I remember interrupting Jerry and saying that I was thinking of running for the US Congress in 1986 "So that people don't forget me and I can stay relevant in the political game." Jerry looked at me very seriously and said; "You don't get it Steve. Your losing is your opportunity to try something outside of elected office and to use your skills in building something different. To build a career outside of elected politics." I was very skeptical. You see, my mentor Jerry Grecco had confidence in me that I clearly didn't have in myself. To actually have a different career path than the one I was convinced and confident that I was destined to succeed in.

Ironically, at about the same time, my academic mentor, Dr. Norman Samuels, then the provost at Rutgers University, suggested that I teach at the University, pursue my doctorate, and start a public affairs television series out of Rutgers. With mixed feelings I decided to do just that, and my first sponsor / funder of that television series was Jerry Grecco, who at the time was a top executive at First Fidelity Bank. Candidly, I wasn't all that confident that I would ever earn a doctorate or succeed in a broadcasting career. Again, luck matters, as does timing. At the same time, the then president of the PBS Flagship station in New York, WNET, Dr. Bill Baker (who is credited for discovering and helping Oprah Winfrey go from being a local reporter in Baltimore to an international superstar and icon) offered me the opportunity to take our public affairs television series called, "Caucus: New Jersey," to the PBS Flagship station in New York City, WNET/Thirteen. Dr. Baker trusted me and our very small neophyte team with a half-hour in the PBS broadcast schedule. Again, he had confidence in my ability in an arena that I had virtually no experience in and very little confidence. That opportunity Bill Baker gave me, along with the support and guidance from Jerry Grecco and Norman Samuels, dramatically changed the course of my professional career.

You see, here's the point. As is the case with many of you reading this right now, others' belief in me gave me confidence that I would never have had alone. My confidence up to that point was exclusively tied to the results of my efforts as opposed to taking a more mature and comprehensive view of confidence. Even the best leaders who see themselves as confident—sometimes need to have their confidence validated. Without the advice and feedback from others we respect and trust—we can become myopic and just a bit insecure. Even the best leaders who see themselves as supremely confident are bolstered by others they trust and respect. I share this detailed example about a less than secure and successful time in my life because it highlights and reminds me of how many times my own confidence level was pretty low. Truth is, at the time, I was downright scared, insecure, vulnerable, and convincing myself that I "didn't have what it took to succeed." I came to realize that my lack of confidence, along with a sense of fear and anxiety, was largely a product of how I chose to see my situation—the loss of an election. (A bad "result.") This is something I see in so many of our leadership coaching clients today. Their lack of confidence is largely about how they choose to see the situation or an outcome. They convince themselves that the situation defines them and their effort, which is largely negative.

Losing Doesn't Make You a "Loser"

Since that "loss" in the state legislature, I've lost a communication column in "The Star-Ledger", (the largest newspaper in New Jersey when newspapers mattered a lot more) I've lost several TV gigs with major broadcast networks, I was fired by ABC, my contract was not renewed at MSNBC, I've lost certain major sponsors of our PBS broadcasting, not to mention some Stand & Deliver clients—and oh yeah, my doctoral dissertation defense was rejected several times by my dissertation committee, until my dissertation chairman and mentor, Dr. Jorge Schement, gave me the confidence to go on and pass the finish line and receive my doctorate. Oh, I forgot, my first book, *Speak from the Heart*, was rejected by a dozen publishers until Simon and Schuster published it in 2002. You see, the point is, every time I feel down or experience a rejection or loss, I realized that my lack of confidence was how I chose to see the situation. It sounds so simplistic but losing doesn't mean you are a loser. Being defeated in a particular situation doesn't make you a defeated person. And, being rejected doesn't have to mean you are rejected across the board. Confidence in leadership and in life is largely a product of understanding that rejection, coming up short, flopping, and what others perceive as failure, is really an opportunity to learn, grow, pivot, adapt and get better moving forward. It is also an opportunity to practice, which doesn't make perfect, but does make progress and isn't that what leadership is all about? Simply put, I believe in the late, great, college coach Jim Valvano's motto that he shared at the 1993 ESPY Awards, "Don't give up. Don't ever give up!"

With this backdrop in mind and hearing about the many times that didn't work out for me as I hoped or planned, consider some of the keys to becoming a more confident leader. Confident not because you think you are the best, but because you consistently strive to be the best you can be knowing that perfection doesn't exist, but progress and growth in itself, is the ultimate goal.

Don't give into the "imposter syndrome." Of course, many of us think we are playing over our heads in certain situations but realize that a lot of people in the room may feel the same way. My advice? Even when you are feeling just a bit insecure, "act as if" you belong in the room because the more you do that the more confident and comfortable you will become in the process.

Imagine there is a fork in the road and the road to the left is filled with insecurity and fear. I call that the "what if" road. What if this or that goes wrong? What if I make a mistake? What if I leave something out in my presentation? What if they don't like or respect me? Instead, take the road to the right, which I call the helpful road. This simply means that I have passion and I am confident that I have great passion for others and making a difference and adding value in a particular situation. Focus on how you can be of service to others in your leadership, because the more you do that, the more confident you will be in your efforts.

Get Comfortable Being Uncomfortable

Learn to "get comfortable being uncomfortable." Many of our clients tell me I am "uncomfortable presenting in front of others." I get it, I understand, but until you lean into that feeling of being uncomfortable and power through it, you won't build your confidence when presenting to others. Don't let your uncomfortable feelings stop you from trying to do something that you've convinced yourself you are "just not good at." It is a mind game. The more you work through those feelings of being uncomfortable, the more confident you will become moving forward. Your vulnerability—and your willingness to recognize it, is actually a leadership attribute.

Accept that you are going to fall off the bike. Even the most confident leaders make mistakes. Accept it and see it as an opportunity to learn and grow from those mistakes or so-called "failures." This has everything to do with building more confidence, not that you are perfect and never make mistakes, but rather that you are confident that you will constantly learn and grow and get better as a leader. It is a different way of looking at confidence and leadership, but one that is more in line with the reality that none of us are prefect leaders because perfect leadership just doesn't exist.

Practice Makes Progress...Not Perfect

Have a short memory. The great Yankee relief pitcher Mariano Rivera had a very short memory. What does that mean? While most times he came into a game and struck people out with ease, there were times he would get hit hard and the Yankees would lose. According to Rivera, the key to his success was to have a "very short memory," meaning, he would get that bad experience out of his mind quickly and be anxious to get out there again on the mound. The same thing is true with leadership. Learn from our mistakes, but don't obsess over them. A short memory is key to confident leadership. Remember that practice makes progress, not perfect, because the more you imagine there is such a thing as a perfect leader, the less confident you will be. Rather, be confident about your progress and your commitment to growth as a leader because the status quo is never a really good option.

Chapter 6
"Strategic Micromanaging": No Detail Too Small

When we refer to "micromanaging" we mean versus "trusting your people to do the job" by effective delegating. I have been thinking an awful lot about these issues lately. I am an admitted "micromanager" in certain situations. Yet, micromanaging and effective strategic leadership are rarely used in the same sentence. In my coaching, teaching and writing, I often advocate the importance of leaders having a strategic "bigger vision" and the need to "see the forest from the trees." Clearly, that's still true. Leaders must practice the Jim Collins' book *Good to Great* "bus driver" analogy of knowing exactly where the bus is going and why the bus is going there. That is strategic. However, I've seen and coached too many leaders who make the mistake of thinking that because they've set a clear and strategic direction and communicated what needs to be done and why, that somehow it is magically going to be executed as planned. That's a good one! It only works...sometimes...in the military.

Further, the issue of leaders being actively engaged in logistics is extremely important, particularly in the age of COVID-19 and beyond. Why do I say this? Well, just think about the importance of our federal leaders, scientists and public health leaders who were engaged in "Operation Warp Speed" throughout most of 2020 and coming up with extremely effective (but not perfect) vaccines to fight COVID-19. Clearly, it was important and necessary and it was a life-altering accomplishment that gave all of us reason for hope against a deadly global pandemic. Now, consider the vaccine roll-out, especially in the early days. The logistics. It was chaotic, confusing, haphazard, and a national embarrassment. (Clearly, much progress was made in the months after.) The reasons for this are many, but coordinating logistics was and is a part of vaccine distribution—not to mention vaccine's resistance and / or acceptance. Yet, strategic micromanaging and getting "in the weeds" was critically important, not just while the vaccine was being developed, but while monitoring vaccine distribution, promoting vaccine acceptance and tracking it along the way, including an early and effective comprehensive public awareness campaign.

One of the books that has impacted me deeply is the late Richard Carlson's, *Don't Sweat the Small Stuff* series. Carlson talks about the need for all of us to have more patience and not over-react to the "small stuff." He says to ask ourselves, "Will this matter a year from now?" While the book was published in 1997 and remains in a prominent place in my leadership library for reference, I find myself rethinking the limitations of the so-called "small stuff" theory. As leaders, we can't overreact or lose our cool (which I have done on too many occasions). I find myself often frustrated with the so-called "little things" that go wrong, including situations in which team members (or consider the last contractor you hired to renovate your home) who just don't get it right. As a leader, I have given direction, coached and provided feedback to team members, yet too often the execution falls short or is less than optimal. I'm not talking about perfection, but rather excellence. I've tried to be patient but I often fall short in this area. I admit it. My frustration has gotten the best of me and I have talked to Mary about this at length. "Is it me, Mary? I just don't get it. What am I doing wrong?" Sometimes I feel like banging my head against the wall.

Excellence is Not Negotiable

There is no doubt about it, as is the case with many leaders, I lead a terrific team with dedicated professionals who care a lot, but on too many occasions, mistakes have been made based on leaders simply not checking or following up and following through or accepting a work product that in my view is simply not good enough. It is not excellence. My concern is that simply saying leaders shouldn't "sweat the small stuff" can send the message that mediocrity or less than an excellent performance is acceptable. The problem is that in my leadership coaching I have come to believe that "The standard of excellence is not negotiable." Mediocrity or the status quo should never be acceptable. Yes, leaders need to be patient with team members who lack the experience or expertise to execute at the highest level. Patience is a leadership virtue. But over time, if the leader has coached, given feedback, coached again, given more feedback and is sufficiently patient—at a certain point strategic micromanaging is the only reasonable option, other than escorting said team member off the bus.

To be blunt, my concern is that just "trusting" people regardless of the goal you are trying to achieve, too often feels like a lazy, passive and disengaged leadership approach to me. Not a malicious lazy, but attention to detail lazy. In my book, *Lessons in Leadership*, I wrote that in 2010, President Barack Obama was focused on getting the much-needed Affordable Care Act passed. He delegated the "details" of how the website, healthcare.gov, was supposed to function and operate as the primary tool to access the program, but his team simply didn't do the job. I've said then, and I'll say again, it wasn't President Obama's job to build, develop and coordinate the website, but it wasn't enough to simply trust that those he delegated the job to would execute as needed. This approach often proves weak and insufficient. Yet, whether it is the early stages of the the COVID-19 vaccine rollout or the healthcare.gov launch debacle, the important lesson for leaders is that we understand there is an important and critical role we must play in following up and following through on the details and yes, at times, getting "in the weeds" with team members. About what? About what exactly will be done (or not) by when, by whom, and then verifying exactly what progress had been made or not. In turn, leaders must then intervene and artfully confront, coach, support and challenge team members when performance falls short or issues of logistics arise.

Trust, But Verify (Or, Verify and Trust More)

When leaders ignore or minimize strategic micromanaging or believe that they don't need to take this assertive and more engaged approach or believe somehow it is not their job to be so involved, they pay a hefty price when projects fail. For years, Mary and I have had ongoing discussions about "trusting our people" and she has often said to me that there is a healthier balance to my, "I assume it is not going to be done until you prove otherwise to me," approach. As I've stated, trust but verify. This has been my leadership philosophy for years. So, instead of asking; "Do you understand what needs to be done?" which clarifies nothing and in fact can contribute to confusion and miscommunication, rather ask; "Tell me exactly how you are going to accomplish XYZ." This will give you the opportunity to verify what is understood, what isn't, what is confused and what needs to be clarified by you as a leader / coach. Only then, in this effort to "verify," what a team member plans on doing can you begin to create more trust. Further, when said team member consistently executes in that fashion achieving the desired result will that trust grow. I know that there are flaws in every leadership approach, but I guess I have had too many contractors that we've hired in our home to do renovations who haven't done what they promised they were going to do by a certain time, not to mention falling short on quality. As I said, I call it the "trust but verify" philosophy.

When it comes to organizational life, consider that there have been too many e-mails, contracts and letters that have gone out over my signature with typos, incorrect information and frankly, things that reflect poorly on any organization or its leader. When things like this go wrong, it is the team leader's job to take full responsibility. Call it "extreme ownership." So, while never throwing anyone on the team under the bus with outside stakeholders, like any leader, I can get frustrated in that I trust that our people care deeply about their work and our mission—however, I don't always trust that their work is right or that they recognize that they don't know what they don't know. For leaders, saying "I trust" my people sounds great. But I argue that trust when it comes to performance and execution is a more complicated reality.

So, here's what I've seen. If I don't strategically micromanage the external communication on behalf of our organization or the work product put out by our public broadcasting production company on the air, I consider that to be poor leadership. This so-called "hands off" approach has the potential to have too many important things slip through the cracks. Of course, when the same team members consistently deliver an excellent work product, such strategic micromanaging must still be practiced but not to the same degree—moderation matters. The same is true for our leadership firm Stand & Deliver, which is managed by my very able colleague Mary Gamba, which allows me to engage in a lot less micromanaging because she is as obsessed about the little things as I am.

The Best Leaders Are "Responsible" for Everything in Their Universe

Remember, this leadership approach doesn't mean I am supposed to do everyone's job, but I am responsible for the job that everyone does or doesn't do. Balance matters as well. So, it pushes me to be a strategic micromanager and adhere to the "no detail too small" leadership approach while still trying to be a strategic big-picture leader and visionary. Finally, as I've stated, at times, this approach to leading can be incredibly challenging and frustrating to those around you. Yet, while no leadership approach is perfect, this approach has served me well and more importantly helped our team achieve a significant degree of success and excellence.

Chapter 7
What's Up with these "Leaky Bags of Sh*t"?

Facilitating seminars and coaching always teaches me something new about leadership and communication. This revelation brings to mind a leadership seminar I was facilitating recently with the International Union of Engineers (IUOE) Local 825. Greg Lalevee is the Business Manager for the IUOE Local 825, and is a good friend, client and someone who thinks an awful lot about leadership. He has appeared with Mary and me on our "Lessons in Leadership" syndicated series on many occasions. (Log on to Stand-Deliver.com to see past episodes of Lessons in Leadership.)

In a particular seminar in late 2020, while discussing certain frustrations many leaders deal with involving the performance of team members, Greg brought up his concerns about team members sometimes bringing him problems, dumping them on his lap, and expecting him to "fix" things simply because he holds the highest position in the org chart.

What IS A "Leaky Bag?"

In very graphic and in some ways amusing terms, Greg explained his "leaky bag of sh*t" theory. Says Greg, "To me, it's don't walk in with a problem without walking in with a couple of different possible solutions to the problem, willing to talk about it as the leader. But to just drop the problem, like a leaky bag of sh*t, and walk out, assumes an awful lot. I have the time to address the problem. I have the resources to address the problem. I even know the answer to the problem because a good leader realizes that he or she doesn't have the answer to every question. So, it takes time and effort, but I ask my team members to walk in with solutions to the problem that they see."

Wow. There it is. Greg Lalevee's frustration will be familiar to most leaders reading this. Have you ever heard a leader say don't bring me a problem unless you have a solution? While I relate to this philosophy, I take a slightly different approach. My only concern is that this message runs the risk of discouraging team members from bringing problems to you because too often the "solution" isn't so clear cut. But, as I listened to Greg's "leaky bag" theory and thought more about it, I have come to this conclusion. Before you go to your team leader in a knee-jerk fashion by saying, "Hey boss, we have a problem," team members need to actually think, brainstorm, consider possible options and, yes, potential solutions. That doesn't mean that they know exactly what to do, but they have thought about it. They have pondered it. They have struggled with it, instead of simply dumping it in the team leader's lap.

Coach Your People to Think "Possible Solutions"

So, why doesn't this happen more often? My theory is many team members have what I call the "I am not the leader, you are" philosophy. This could result from a combination of factors, including fear (of the unknown), a lack of confidence or an organizational culture that fails to promote the empowerment of each team member and encouraging them to step up and lead. The problem is people say, "I am not the leader, you are," it just won't get most teams where they need to be in a highly competitive, fast-changing, evolving environment with intense competition. That approach won't work on the best teams—the teams that have to be innovative, creative, entrepreneurial and ultimately successful. What I am advocating and what Greg Lalevee implied with his pithy "leaky bags of sh*t" analogy is that ultimately, on the best teams, "everyone is a leader" (see our chapter entitled "Everyone is a Leader," which comes from our good friend and former NJ Resources CEO Larry Downes.)

Okay—then what exactly is the job of the team leader? I argue that the team leader should take his or her frustration around receiving so-called "leaky bags" and channel it into asking strategic and probing questions of team members and helping them to be the most effective leaders they can be. As most people know who have read my previous books on leadership and communication and are familiar with the series Mary and I co-anchor called, "Lessons in Leadership," my approach is to describe my own shortcomings as a leader and what I have learned in the process. In this regard, I have been guilty of being a less than effective leader when having a so-called "leaky bag of sh*t" dumped in my lap. I admit I have a "fix it" mentality. I am pretty sure it is in my genetic makeup. That is who my father was as a leader and I've come to realize that basically I enjoy "fixing things," being the one to solve the problem and, on some level, basking in the fact that "I was the one that figured it out." (I know, an issue to be discussed in therapy!)

The "Fix It" Leader...

The problem is that in many ways this is a flawed leadership approach. It is leadership driven too much by ego and frustration. Further, it potentially creates unintended consequences. Consider; if a leader is the "Mr. / Mrs. Fix It" that team members come to expect he or she will simply "fix any problem," said leader discourages others from thinking for themselves. The leader lowers expectations for every team member by not challenging them to be more creative, entrepreneurial and strategic in their thinking and collaborating with others by coming up with options as to how to deal with particularly difficult situation. This can create a "top down" organizational culture that does not promote an entrepreneurial, innovative and problem-solving spirit.

It is similar to what some of us as "helicopter parents" have done with our kids. They have a problem, one that often they have created out of immaturity, laziness, lack of experience, and we "fix it." No matter what happens, mom and dad will fix it for them. I am definitely guilty in this regard, as is my wife, Jennifer. When we do this too often with our kids, what are we teaching them? No matter what happens, we will "fix it" for them. In turn, what motivation do our children have to think for themselves, to be more accountable and responsible for the problems that they create or are confronted with? I am not saying that members in an organization are exactly like our teenage children, but there are some similarities. As leaders, we must fight the urge, even if you think you have a solution, to jump in and "fix it" in every case. We need to resist the urge to swoop in on our "leadership helicopter" and solve every problem without engaging team members and asking questions and challenging their thinking as to what options may be available to them. I know...easier said than done!

As leaders, we must help our team members be the leaders they are capable of being, even if they tell you at first that they are not leaders, but they are willing to follow direction. That is not enough. As leaders we must encourage collaboration, brainstorming and yes, the struggle of team members thinking through a problem and presenting possible options and solutions. Does it take longer and can it be frustrating? Yes. But the long-term reward of leading in this fashion is that we help our team members become a better version of themselves. Does it make them uncomfortable at times? No doubt, but it is a "good uncomfortable" because they are thinking, they are engaged and ultimately if they are in fact part of the solution because of their efforts, they are clearly more invested in the organization and the decisions that are made in how to handle particularly sticky problems. This approach will also help you to build your organization's succession planning efforts. Is any of this easy? Of course not, but as I have said on many occasions, leadership, at least the kind I am describing, is not for everyone. But for those of us who try to practice this leadership on a daily basis, in spite of the frustrations, it is extremely gratifying.

Chapter 8
Grit: The *Really* Tough Stuff

Why "Jimmy V's" ESPY Speech Still Matters

"Don't give up. Don't ever give up!" Those were the powerful words of the late great college basketball coach Jim Valvano as he was honored at the 1993 ESPY Awards. Valvano knew he was dying from an incurable and aggressive form of cancer. I wrote about "Jimmy V," as he was known, in the original *Lessons in Leadership book*, praising him for his extraordinary public speaking ability to move, motivate and inspire others. But in this chapter on grit, I look at coach Jimmy V from a different perspective.

In March 1993, physically, Jim Valvano was a shell of the full of life, overjoyed, 1983 NCAA-Championship-winning basketball coach. I'll never forget on the night NC State won the NCAA Championship, the chaotic scene of Coach Valvano—running wildly all over the court as the final buzzer went off. His team had won in the last second and the coach was just looking for someone to hug—to celebrate with—to rejoice in finally reaching the pinnacle of the college basketball world. That was Jimmy V. He never stopped talking, back slapping or hugging. He was an animated Italian-America guy from Brooklyn who people gravitated toward, yet just 10-years after winning the NCAA Championship, there was Jimmy V—being helped on and off the stage during the 1993 ESPY's. Valvano died the month after the ESPY's, on April 28, 1993, at only 47 years of age.

Jim Valvano was a charismatic leader. A motivator of young men. A great fundraiser for his program. A basketball genius with a winning personality. Yet, what Jimmy V had more than anything else was and abundance of GRIT! A steely determination to "never give up" and fight to the end—regardless of the odds. By any normal or reasonable standard, Valvano wasn't supposed to even be able to attend the 1993 Espy Awards. He was clearly at death's door. He could barely walk. Yet, Jimmy V willed himself to sit through a long ceremony and then get helped up the steps to the microphone and deliver the most memorable sports related speech in modern history. Sure, his words mattered a lot. But it was who was saying them that mattered so much more.

Jim Valvano isn't the only great leader who has made his mark by having an extraordinary amount of grit. Yet before I discuss some examples of grit, let's explore this grit thing a bit further. In her book, **GRIT: *The Power of Passion and Perseverance***, author Angela Duckworth, a professor of psychology at University of Pennsylvania, examined the attributes of leaders and professionals in their respective fields. While "talent" or natural ability mattered a lot, Duckworth concluded the following:

> "The highly accomplished were paragons of perseverance. Why were the highly accomplished so dogged in their pursuits? For most, there was no realistic expectation of ever catching up to their ambitions. In their own eyes, they were never good enough. They were the opposite of complacent. And yet, in a very real sense, they were satisfied being unsatisfied. Each was chasing something of unparalleled interest and importance, and it was the chase—as much as the capture—that was gratifying. Even if some of the things they had to do were boring, or frustrating, or even painful, they wouldn't dream of giving up. Their passion was enduring.
>
> In sum, no matter the domain, the highly successful had a kind of ferocious determination that played out in two ways. First, these exemplars were unusually resilient and hardworking. Second, they knew

in a very, very deep way what it was they wanted. They not only had determination, they had direction. It was this combination of passion and perseverance that made high achievers special. In a word, they had grit." [1]

To add more perspective on this subject, consider the words of leadership guru John Maxwell; "Grit many times wins over the best.... Grit wins, almost always, over giftedness. Grit takes you where others don't go.... It's that grit that'll get you to the finish line."

Having Grit Doesn't Make You Fearless

Grit is a funny thing. Some people mistakenly believe it is about simply being fearless—leaders who just believe that they can do anything—regardless of the obstacles they face. My view of grit, especially as it relates to leadership, is a bit different. In many cases, I'm convinced that exceptional leaders with genuine grit do in fact experience some level of fear—self-doubt—and vulnerability. Yet, despite all this, these people—these leaders—persevere and refuse to give up—they refuse to give in to those very real emotions, feelings and fear. The truly great leader is not someone who is never afraid. He is the leader who may in fact be afraid or vulnerable, but chooses to do the strong and courageous thing anyway. He takes the action he knows is harder and will potentially be more painful because he refuses to give in and refuses to give up. In many cases, the reward for exhibiting such grit is great success. What makes these leaders different is that they allow themselves to have and to experience their fear; they just don't let it stop them from moving forward.

Gritty Leaders Refuse to Be Victims

Grit is about after getting knocked down, having no choice but to get back up again, again and again. It is about resilience and resourcefulness. It is about refusing to be a victim. I'm not saying these leaders with tons of grit never feel sorry for themselves. Of course they

---

1. ©Angela Duckworth, 2016 *Grit; The Power of Passion and Perseverance*

do. It's just that the "pity party" doesn't last that long. I am not saying this grit thing is easy or that anyone in a leadership position should simply *will* themselves to get grittier. Clearly, in some cases, issues of mental and emotional health come into play. Some people who are suffering from clinical depression and/or crippling anxiety and simply can't always will themselves to tough it out.

Yet, for many of us, grit is a choice. It is a decision. It is a frame of mind. Nobody bats 1,000 when it comes to grit, but over time, the best leaders build grit into their leadership DNA and make it a major component of their leadership toolkit. It's what they rely on when the "tough stuff" comes calling—a global pandemic. an economic downturn. a major business failure. a war in which you are leading a team, or a country being invaded by others. a divorce. a serious health issue. a very public rejection. The list goes on.

As for the "tough stuff" leaders face on a regular basis, I'm not convinced that grit is simply a question of having it or not. Being born with it or not. Is some of it genetic? I imagine, but it doesn't really matter, since there is nothing you can do about your genetics. (I know because, like so many others, I have inherited certain less-than-desirable genetics from my father that I am less than thrilled about. LOL.) One thing I've learned about really strong leaders when it comes to grit is that they don't obsess over what they can't control but rather put all of their energy and passion into what they can—if not control—at least influence and greatly impact. Consider a few examples of leaders and others with lots of grit who inspire us to deal with our own "tough stuff" to be the best leaders possible:

Eric LeGrand, a former Rutgers University football star on the rise, was paralyzed during a 2010 game against Army. Eric was an NFL prospect; a football star on the rise. But in a moment, Eric LeGrand's football career was over. I have come to know and respect Eric over the past decade through a series of interviews on public broadcasting, and I admire the fact that his only obsession is about what he can do versus what has been taken away from him and what he can't do. Today, Eric is an accomplished author, entrepreneur, advocate for the Christopher and Dana Reeve Foundation and radio broadcaster for Rutgers football. Eric has a degree of grit most of us just can't comprehend. Yes, he is paralyzed in a wheelchair, but he is convinced that one day he will walk again. If you knew Eric LeGrand, and his grit, you wouldn't bet against him.

Randy Pausch, the author of *The Last Lecture*, had a different kind of grit. In 2007, Randy Pausch, a professor at Carnegie Mellon University, knew he had terminal cancer, but like Jim Valvano, highlighted earlier in this chapter, Randy Pausch decided that he wanted to use his limited days on this earth to make a difference. In his iconic "last lecture" at Carnegie Mellon, he motivated and inspired millions not only through his best-selling book, but through a memorable appearance on Oprah (when Oprah's talk show was "must-watch" TV). His message was about living and appreciating every day on this earth, making a difference in the lives of others, giving back and simply choosing to be happy. Randy passed away in July 2008, but his "last lecture" and his inspiring powerful lessons live on. No one will ever question Randy Pausch's grit.

Rosa Parks is everything that grit looks like. During one of the worst periods in American history in which blacks faced devastating discrimination—especially in the South—Rosa Parks simply refused to sit in the back of the bus as laws stated in several states in the South. It was Rosa Parks who came to symbolize the fight for civil rights and equality. She didn't scream; she didn't yell; she didn't stomp her feet. She just stood firm in quietly leading by her actions and, in turn, motivating and inspiring others in more powerful positions in government to change laws, as well as influencing hearts and minds across America when it came to the issue of race race relations and civil rights.

Prime Minister Winston Churchill had his back against the wall in England as the Nazis were invading, moving violently through Europe at a record pace. While many leaders across the globe, including some in the U.S., were leery of challenging Hitler and his diabolical and deadly actions, Churchill stood strong. He inspired and motivated others to be braver and stronger than they ever thought they could be. England stood up to Hitler. None of that would have happened if Winston Churchill, despite all of his flaws (like any leader) didn't have an extraordinary amount of grit. In March of 2022, some of this same grit, tenacity and courage is being demonstrated by Ukrainian President Volodymyr Zelensky. It's odd, because Zelensky, before facing this horrific and vicious attack by Vladimir Putin and the Russian army, was an actor and comedian. There was no logical reason to believe he could and would be a great leader, but as of this writing, he has been a leader in a way that no one could have imagined. This is a classic example of certain individuals rising to the occasion and demonstrating extraordinary leadership and revealing tremendous grit because of the situation before them. That's what Winston Churchill had in the early 1940s during WWII and what President Volodymyr Zelensky as well as the people of Ukraine have shown in the face of a brutal Russian assault.

Lou Gehrig. As an iconic Yankee star in the 1920s and 1930s, Lou Gehrig played alongside Babe Ruth. Gehrig was known as the "Iron Horse" because he was strong, resilient, and played in virtually every game. No days off. And then in the prime of his career, he was stricken with a horrific disease (now known as ALS), which debilitated him. That didn't stop Gehrig from delivering the most memorable and inspiring speech at Yankee Stadium upon his retirement, which moved many to tears. In that speech, Lou Gehrig, dying from this debilitating illness, would call himself, "The luckiest man on the face of the earth." He was referring to his relationships and friendships throughout his baseball career in Yankee pinstripes. That's grit. That's courage. That was Lou Gehrig.

St. Peter's University Peacocks: Jersey City Grit. A small college in Jersey City in 2022 went deep into the NCAA basketball tournament, beating much larger and established basketball teams such as Kentucky, Purdue, Murray State. They were undermanned and underfunded, but led by their coach Shaheen Holloway, who has since returned to his alma mater at Seton Hall University), the St. Peter's Peacocks shocked the college basketball world with their grit, toughness, and a belief in themselves that has become part of college basketball history.

So, finally, let's break down some of the most significant traits of the grittiest leaders.

Resilience. The ability to bounce back after getting knocked down. It is simply refusing to give in or give up no matter what the odds or how many times we fall short.

Passion. The grittiest leaders care deeply, not just about what they do but about its impact on others. They care deeply about their leadership craft, their art, their specialty, whatever that may be. But they also have tremendous passion about pursuing excellence and the highest standards in their respective fields.

No excuses. Gritty leaders simply don't make excuses. They don't blame others or point fingers. Yes, there are often extenuating or unique and difficult circumstances, but gritty leaders don't use this to focus on what they can't do but instead have a laser-like focus on what they can and will do to make a less than optimal situation better.

Ego and pride. Ego isn't always a bad thing for a leader, especially if one's ego causes them to have tremendous pride in what they do and how they perform. That combination of ego and pride can produce a degree of grit that will often help a leader get through the toughest stuff he or she will inevitably face.

Intense competitiveness. I'm not necessarily referring to comparing yourself to others, but rather constantly competing against yourself, comparing yourself to your previous performance as a leader. This intense sense of competition and drive to be better is essential to great leadership. Gritty leaders never accept the status quo, and they push themselves outside their comfort zone in an effort to grow and improve.

Fail forward. Seeing "losing" as an opportunity to learn. Falling short, getting rejected, coming in 2nd, gritty leaders just see these outcomes as an opportunity to grow and learn from past mistakes or missteps. Gritty leaders see "losing" as the fuel that drives them toward excellence.

So, for leaders who want to be at their best, grit—as described in this chapter—is an absolute necessity. It's not something that is just nice to have, it is a requirement and for those who think that grit is something only a select few have, I say dig deeper and tap into the grit that I'm confident is just below the surface. It's there, trust me, and trust yourself.

Chapter 9

The Most Important F Words:
"Forced Engagement" and Facilitation

Throughout the COVID-19 pandemic, as well as when we get back to the so called "new normal," great leaders MUST assertively engage others. I'm not sure whether we should call it "forced engagement," because Mary has communicated to me that just using the word "forced" is problematic. She says it potentially sends an unnecessarily confrontational message. Yet, I am torn, because I actually do believe as leaders we sometimes, in certain situations, must be really assertive, bordering on forcing participation and engagement of others.

What Is "Forced" Engagement?

Why must leaders force engagement and what exactly does engaging people really mean? Think about it. Consider how many Zoom meetings you have been in, and how often you were some combination of bored, disinterested, engaged in multi-tasking, texting, e-mailing and doing a variety of other things while this so-called meeting was going on. Why is that? Clearly, you were not fully engaged. The leader of the meeting didn't pull you in, didn't call you by name and ask you a question, or didn't push you to share your opinion or perspective. In turn, the meeting leader didn't follow up on something you said because they wanted to know more or get others to respond to your perspective. As a result, you didn't feel invested enough in that meeting or conversation to be thinking, sharing, listening and actively participating.

However, it's not just meetings in which leaders must engage participants, but rather in virtually in everything we do. Too often, leadership is seen by too many as simply directing other people to do specific things. This "command and control" approach to leadership does work and is appropriate in certain situations, such as in a high-pressured, time-sensitive law-enforcement scenario, or a fire, crisis or other disaster. Command and control leadership has its place. However, these situations are not the norm and too many of us as leaders are not prepared to or committed to getting other people talking. I have come to call this "forced engagement", but like I said, this phrase is one my colleague Mary Gamba doesn't particularly like, and prefers to call it assertive, compelled or "active engagement." But regardless of what you call it, the status quo for most leaders when it comes to getting others involved and engaged simply isn't working in the vast majority of cases.

"Putting People on the Spot" Or... "Inviting Them In?"

About a year into the pandemic, I noticed that our older son, Nick, who was a senior in high school at the time, was in bed participating in a virtual class, in his pajamas, at about 11 a.m. Later in the day I asked him, "Nick, how can you be in class while lying in bed?" His response was revealing, "Dad, it's not as if the teachers call on you and it doesn't really matter because I am taking notes on what is being said." My response, "Nick, are you really saying the teacher doesn't call you out by name and ask what your lesson or take away was from a particular chapter that you read for that specific class?" His response spoke volumes, "Dad, most teachers don't do that." "Why not Nick?" "Well, not everyone puts people on the spot the way you do!"

So, there it is. Asking people questions, by name, is considered "putting people on the spot". We are not just talking about my son Nick. I have heard the "putting people on the spot" explanation by countless, much older, corporate managers who run meetings in very much the same way too many of our teachers teach. Think about it. How is it that we define asking people questions to get their input and invite them to share their perspective as "putting them on the spot?" Wouldn't a team benefit from hearing what other team members are thinking? How will we share ideas and think about difficult and challenging issues in our workplace if we do not assertively and, yes, forcefully engage all team members? I just don't see how that is possible.

Leadership IS Facilitation

Now let's talk about the other "f-word," facilitation. Even if you don't like the term "forced engagement," leaders must ask themselves exactly how they will actively create an environment in which engagement is the norm and not the exception? As leaders, we must see ourselves as facilitators. In this role, we must "force" engagement. Consider this sports analogy. It is like a point guard in basketball or a quarterback in football. Your job is to move the team forward and put team members in the best position to succeed. As a point guard, you pass the ball around and keep things moving in a coordinated, dynamic and productive fashion. It is the same with a quarterback. It is also similar to a traffic cop who keeps things moving on our streets. This isn't some abstract theory I've developed that hasn't been tested time and time again, but rather a very practical approach to how I lead meetings, seminars, workshops, panel discussions, as well as with my family— particularly during dinner conversations. (I'm sure others sometimes find this style of engagement irritating, yet I still haven't figured out another way of starting a conversation and getting other people contributing.)

I have had many people initially push back and I know that some were turned off by my asking them a specific question that invites them to participate by sharing their thoughts. My response? That's okay. If you feel "put on the spot" by me asking you a question, my question is, why do you think so little of yourself that what you have to say has no value? Further, I've had clients and students over the years say, "Steve, I'm okay with you asking questions, but not of specific people. Why not just ask the group a question and let someone volunteer to answer who feels confident enough to speak in front of the group?" In theory, that is a terrific idea. But in practice, it doesn't work. Here's why.

Did you ever notice when you do this, the same two or three people answer virtually every question? Yes, it is those who are confident and comfortable to speak up. And what happens to everyone else? They hang back, they check out, they look at their iPhone and start texting and e-mailing. My view? Active facilitation and forced engagement is actually showing tremendous respect for every participant in either a remote or in person interaction. It tells people that you actually care what they think. It pushes people outside their comfort zone to challenge themselves. It creates better decisions for a team by getting the benefit of everyone's thinking and perspectives. But none of this happens without active, sometimes forced engagement and facilitation.

Finally, if you do this enough, and do it in the spirit of collegiality and where there is an, "I want to know what you think" approach, over time a leader can actually create a more engaged culture in an organization. How? By raising the bar for everyone's participation. By letting them know that showing up and just having a pulse isn't going to be enough at your next meeting or brainstorming session, etc. You are letting them know that being prepared to share and speak and really think will be required, as is listening to your colleagues and responding accordingly. Admittedly, this may not be easy for some leaders because for too long too many of us have created a culture where engaging others is not the common practice. Yet, I'm convinced that by learning specific tools of facilitation and engagement—asking probing, open-ended questions—the payoff is more than worth any initial discomfort or awkwardness.

Chapter 10
Why Leaders Must "Artfully Confront"

As leaders, we must confront or "deal with" difficult, challenging and often uncomfortable situations and people. This is so easy to say, and so much harder to do. There is nothing fun about confrontation, but when leaders refuse to or are incapable of dealing with these sticky situations, organizations pay a heavy price. I know from personal and professional experience.

To be clear, I'm not talking about being unnecessarily argumentative or contentious, but rather the kind of thoughtful, courageous and strategic leadership and communication mindset that says; "This is not a good situation. It's been going on for a while, and if I as a leader and we as an organization don't deal with it in a constructive and candid fashion it should have a seriously negative impact on our team."

Sometimes the situation that needs to be confronted involves a team member that, despite consistent coaching, mentoring and patience, just isn't performing at a level the team needs in order to succeed—or is not displaying the necessary cooperation and collaboration. I have coached many clients who have told me that over months, or in some cases, years, that a particular team member isn't "getting the job done." But, when I ask if these leaders want to get this particular team member "off the bus," the response is an emphatic, "Are you kidding me? Of course!"

Yet, when I press the question as to why this unacceptable situation isn't directly confronted, I get weak responses and excuses such as:

> "Steve, do you have any idea how much red tape there is in getting rid of a poor performing team member?"

"I'm going to have to get HR involved and the paperwork is such a pain in the neck. I'll just suck it up."

"Steve, this guy spends more time reading and understanding HR policies on how difficult it is for him to be let go than he does actually doing his job."

"Our underperforming team member is in his early 60s. I don't want to be accused of age discrimination even though his age has nothing to do with it."

"Our organization has a big push on diversity and the team member that isn't getting the job done is our only minority team member. If I let him go, there is going to be tremendous push back and I just don't want to deal with it."

"Bob has been with the company for 30 years and he is well-liked, not to mention he is very close to several senior executives who protect him, even though everyone knows that he is a poor performer, and no one wants him on their team."

And for leaders who must confront difficult and/or unacceptable situations, it could also involve team members who are simply "playing out of position," meaning, they are not right for a particular role on your team. This team member may not have the skills, the inclination, or the mindset to do what the organization needs. From professional experience, I know that I have not effectively confronted situations like this in the past because a particular team member was well-liked by other employees, but I knew instinctively that the team member in question was in fact playing out of position and the team member's skillset just didn't match our organization's needs. In this instance I fell short as a leader and was consistently frustrated much of the time. Consider what would happen if a baseball team is about to enter the World Series and the head coach and manager fail to remove a player that is not in the right position. That leadership failure could torpedo the team's chances of winning the series. Now, think about how this would apply to your organization.

And consider another situation where a team member has the requisite skills and tools and is doing a competent enough job, but his or her overall attitude and demeanor are counterproductive and disruptive to the team. This person is not the best team player, by a long shot. Yet, this employee virtually never volunteers to step up or deal with or help with any challenges that arise. He or she reminds everyone what their role is (and is not) and even if the team needs the team member to go beyond this, it is either done reluctantly or it is not done at all. Again, these difficult and very unacceptable situations must be confronted by the team leader because if they are not, it will impact the morale of other team members, overall team productivity and frankly has a negative impact on the leader's psyche. It can also cause the team leader to lash out and contentiously bicker with others, which is often counterproductive and destructive to the overall team.

Another area that leaders must confront involves fiscal challenges or budgetary realities. Consider that when COVID became very real for most of us in March of 2020, Mary and I had to deal with the fact that the budget of our not-for-profit organization needed to be reduced by several hundred thousand dollars—quickly. It didn't take a genius to realize that the corporations and foundations that support our programming on broadcasting would be losing revenue and many were laying people off. In turn, this would have a potential negative impact on their sponsorship of the kind of programming we were putting on the air—particularly in public broadcasting.

To be as strategic as possible, we had to confront the reality that we would not be recording in our regular studio and needed to gear up for an entirely remote production operation. This remote model would need to be much more streamlined and efficient, but this change would create issues of quality that would become very real. We had to consistently confront the fact that we did not have the team members with the expertise to get the job done as quickly and efficiently as needed, and our team members stepped up to recruit and assemble such a remote production team.

In the process of pivoting and innovating, mistakes were made and there were regular tweaks and adjustments to our remote broadcast look and overall quality. And, yes, throughout I was what I have called in this book a "strategic micromanager," as the team leader responsible for what we put out on the air. I offered my feedback about our lighting, audio quality, set design and, in all candor how I felt I looked in this new and at times confusing, "COVID impacted," production model. There were weekend and late-night e-mails from me about where I felt we needed to "confront" in order to move toward the excellent production that we all knew needed to be achieved.

A Culture of "Confronting"

I am sure my "confronting" these issues was at times irritating to certain team members who must have thought, "What a pain in the ass Steve is—he is never satisfied..." I tried as our team leader to consistently thank and recognize the tremendous effort and hard work of virtually every team member—but as a leader, I also tried to find a healthy and realistic balance between praising our people yet not avoiding the need to "deal with" what I strongly believed "wasn't good enough" and should be improved. As I write this at the end of 2021 and getting closer to two years into this global pandemic, I am confident that our team and overall productivity and quality is better off. This is largely because of what I like to call a "culture of confronting" situations as well as operational and strategic challenges head on instead of avoiding these issues because it could make some team members uncomfortable and/or cause me, or any team leader, to not be especially popular or well liked in the moment.

Together with Mary, we made the very difficult decision to reduce our personnel expenses. We had to confront the reality that in order to put our organization in a stronger financial position with a very uncertain future, at least one high-level producer on our team had to be let go. Mary and I agreed on who this would be and we confronted it together, even though, in retrospect I realized I didn't have the courage (or the stomach) to do it along. Having Mary on the phone with me was incredibly helpful. (Clearly, if not for COVID, this would have been done in person.) The producer we let go was clearly emotional—rightfully so. Yes, we cut the budget in the process and confronted the need to reassign certain tasks and restructure our team, but this very difficult leadership decision also made it crystal clear that one of the reasons that we don't confront what we need to is because of our fear of how the other person will respond. No one likes this. No one enjoys it. No one wants any part of it. But our organization had to be more fiscally sound in order to not only withstand the initial negative impact of a global pandemic, but also to put us in a position to move forward in a restructured, leaner organizational model that would allow us to flourish moving forward.

Now, consider the following case study that brings many of these issues of "confrontation" into perspective. Several years ago, I was coaching Paul, a 30-year-old bank manager who is well liked, hardworking and respected in his company. Yet, recently Paul's CEO suggested some executive coaching as a way to help him take his skills to the next level.

A little background. While no one questions Paul's willingness to work hard and be a team player, he is reluctant to "step up" as his boss says. When pressed by the executive coach, the boss explains that Paul runs meetings that ramble and are unfocused. "He is such a nice guy. He often seems reluctant to cut people off when they are on a tangent." He also says that when Paul's team fails to come to any consensus or decision, he tends to put that same agenda item off until the next meeting. Over time, these less than stellar leadership and communication skills have hurt Paul's career advancement.

During a recent coaching session, Paul was asked about these issues. His response is revealing. "I am really uncomfortable confronting people. It is not my style to be in someone's face and I don't like it when people do it to me." As the session continued, it became clear that Paul saw "confrontation" as exclusively a negative communication approach. Along with so many other professionals, this bank manager sees confrontation as a form of aggression, as something that makes people uncomfortable. They see confrontation as a battle, a contest, a war fought by combatants who will either win or lose.

The Consequences of NOT Confronting

Clearly, confrontation can be and sometimes is many of these things. But there is another way to look at "confrontational communication" as an opportunity to confront an ongoing problem or challenge head on. To not confront it would mean missing a big opportunity. How many of us have long, simmering below-the-surface feuds going on with people we need to get along with? It could be at work or in your personal life. Your bottled-up frustration and anger are making your life miserable and greatly affecting your productivity. In these situations, you MUST confront things head on.

Consider Paul, our bank manager, who needs to say to his colleagues who refuse to reach a decision on a crucial business matter; "Let's be clear, by not coming to a decision on X we stand to lose a lot of potential revenue. If our team is unwilling or unable to decide, I will do it because the alternative will produce an unacceptable outcome.

When Paul was presented with this more direct communication approach by his executive coach, he said, "I can do that! But that's not being confrontational." Yes, it is! It is confronting your colleagues (or others) with your candid view of a situation. It's confronting by communicating the consequences of our action or inaction. Confrontation in this form is a critical leadership tool.

On a personal level, I encourage you to confront anyone with whom you have long-standing issues or concerns that are truly bothering you. Why not tell your wife or husband or someone close to you; "When I do something extra special for you, and you don't even acknowledge it or say thanks, it makes me feel really lousy." No malice. No animosity. No rancor or battle to fight. Just honest communication about something that matters. That's right, confronting the issue. Think about it. The alternative of ignoring or ducking the situation only makes things worse and gets you more frustrated.

In an effort to have this book be practical and relevant to the very difficult and complex issues that you as a leader must confront, consider the following leadership tips and tools when artfully confronting:

—**Empathize.** Take the time to think about what YOU would want to hear in a similar situation. Imagine what it might be like to receive the difficult information you are about to share. In many cases, when the other person believes that you are making that attempt, they feel appreciative. Again, they are not happy to hear the news, but your effort to empathize will make it just a little more bearable.

—**Manage your emotions.** Regardless of the message you are delivering, emotions can easily become charged. The key is to keep your emotions in check, and if you see the other person starting to get defensive or emotional, navigate the situation carefully by either reframing the discussion or taking a quick pause to the meeting.

—**Be solution-oriented**. Don't criticize or give negative feedback without offering a potential remedy to improve the situation like this; "Mary, I feel that we could have done a much better job on the Johnson report. I suggest that as we move forward, we meet and agree on a strategy before we take any actions..."

—**Have a strategy**. Going into a difficult conversation without a "strategy" is dangerous. Identifying your larger goals and the main message you want to get across are keys to staying focused.

—**Be flexible and agile**. When you anticipate push back, defensiveness, or an outright rejection, you need to be prepared to adapt your conversational strategy accordingly. By simply thinking that things will work out the way you want them to basically means you are not prepared.

—**Use open-ended questions**. Identify 2-3 open-ended questions when facilitating to get the other person talking. The key is not to lecture or do all the talking. Yet, once the other party does start talking, be a good listener and ask probing, clarifying and open-ended questions.

—**Use real life examples**. Use concrete, specific and real-life examples to paint a clearer picture of how you see the situation. Don't assume the other person understands just because you understand.

—**Don't avoid difficult conversations**. There is a price to pay when you don't confront difficult conversations. One of my favorite quotes is, "You can't change what you refuse to confront." Some of my clients claim they are too "nice" to engage in difficult conversations. But the consequences are real when a leader practices avoidance.

Chapter 11
What's This "Hub and Spokes?
Strategic Relationship Building

Leadership is largely about getting difficult but important things done. It's also about moving people to act and about connecting with key stakeholders who matter in your professional universe. It's virtually impossible to be a great leader without being a strategic and intentional builder of RELATIONSHIPS. In my executive coaching work, I ask my clients how they approach relationship building. There is often a long pause or a quizzical look and, in turn, I follow up by asking; "You know, building and strengthening relationships that matter to you and your business?" I often get responses like this; "Steve, it's sort of an organic thing that just happens." Or, "I've never really thought about relationship building in that way." Or, this one that is especially revealing, "I reach out for people when I need or want something!" Ouch!

I'm a big believer in taking a more strategic, methodical and intentional approach to creating and bolstering our business relationships. In my work leading a not-for-profit production company in cooperation with PBS television stations in the New York/New Jersey region, a big part of my job (beyond anchoring several broadcasts) is to raise money. As a leader, I sometimes must do this under a lot of pressure and a great deal of uncertainty (As I write this, we are 2-years into the COVID-19 global pandemic). The only way our production company, the Caucus Educational Corporation, is able to produce, broadcast, distribute and promote our programming on a variety of media platforms, is because together with our fundraising team led by Mary Gamba and our colleague Laura Van Bloem, we work every day on our *relationships* with existing sponsors and underwriters as well as on identifying potential supporters (which means new potential relationships).

We take the same approach to strategic relationship building with our firm, Stand & Deliver, a leadership and communication coaching organization that Mary and I have grown over more than 20 years together. Beyond consistently delivering a quality product (be it a program on PBS or a leadership seminar in person or remotely), any success Mary and I have had at Stand & Deliver is due largely to our business relationships.

It's funny, while I'm calling it a "business relationship," in many ways, these relationships often have a personal or human element to them. These relationships cannot simply be transactional exchanges for them to endure and sustain through difficult and challenging times. These relationships must be more. They must be deeper and more meaningful. Simply put, there must be an element of caring—I'm talking empathy and genuine concern and desire to be helpful and of value to key business stakeholders. As leaders, we must come from a place that always asks; "why does this matter and how does it impact THEM?"

When I use the term "business stakeholder", I am referring to the most important and essential people in your universe who impact your ability to lead and be effective in your role. Again, strengthening your relationship with these key stakeholders shouldn't be managed in a haphazard (some call it organic) fashion. Sure, unexpected opportunities present themselves to bolster a business relationship, and "luck" has its place (right place right time stuff), but real, sustaining relationships in the world of business must be consistently nurtured, maintained and grown.

The Hub and Spokes Strategic Relationship-building Model

Consider what I call the "hub and spokes" strategic relationships building approach. Think of yourself as the "hub" of a bicycle tire and the "spokes" as the key stakeholders or audiences that you must engage and stay connected with—simply put, the folks and/or the organizations (including clients, colleagues, associates, prospects, and investors) that will greatly impact your ability to effectively lead and move your team forward.

This hub and spokes strategic relationship building approach is anything but a "one way street," but rather an "other-centered" two-way highway. Much of your ability to manage this hub and spokes is based on your consistent efforts to genuinely connect with and engage your stakeholders. This can't be done by simply "checking off the box" and telling yourself you must have a specific number of "stakeholder touches" in a given period of time. To me, that is more quantity over quality or, as Mary likes to call it, "more activity over impact."

The hub and spokes strategic relationships building approach I buy into is about the long game. It's about establishing and strengthening real, lasting relationships that endure even in the most challenging of times. This is not an approach to "sales." I say that not because I'm against "selling," but because too often too many "salespeople" focus on getting you to buy something regardless of whether you want or need it. Selling is largely transactional. Too often it is about "hitting your numbers." The kind of strategic relationship building I'm talking about is very different. It requires that you consistently focus on being attentive to your key stakeholders and buying in to the "it's about THEM" philosophy toward business. It's about having empathy for your stakeholders, their reality, their needs, wants and aspirations.

I strongly suggest that you sit down and strategically and methodically identify who your key stakeholders are. Start with your teammates—your professional colleagues. Better yet, in the spirit of practicing a healthier approach to "work-life" integration—start with your family. The key is to build this type of thinking, activity and communication into your everyday life. The goal is to have a hub and spokes relationship-building philosophy engrained into your leadership DNA. With this in mind, consider some of the following real-life, best-practices along with some examples of effective business relationship building.

Be There in Difficult Times

It's easy to have a great business relationship when things are going well for your business stakeholders. Their business is going well, they are giving you and your company business, and everyone is happy. But what about the difficult times when there is an economic downturn or a global pandemic that turns the world upside down and businesses and organizations of every stripe are challenged just to keep their doors open?

A little over a decade ago, a long-time client and friend who was the CEO of a major corporation called me to say that their stock price had dropped dramatically because of serious problems in their industry. He told me that their corporation would no longer be able to sponsor our public broadcasting programming and our leadership development coaching at his company would have to be put on hold. I was clearly disappointed, concerned but at the same time I could hear in my friend's voice that this was incredibly difficult for him. But he made the call. He reached out. He told me directly. While I listened, I also said this to him; "Bob, I can't imagine how hard this must be for you and your colleagues, but why don't we do this? We'll keep the corporation's branding on our program for a few months longer and I will also make myself available to coach any of your senior team members who need my help. This isn't about me being overly altruistic (because trust me, I care about making a good living) but I realized that a long-time business stakeholder, friend and colleague was in a really bad way. He needed to know that I would be there for him.

I remember him being genuinely appreciative and he knew he could reach out to talk any time he needed. The next year things turned for the better, stock prices went up dramatically and the company was stabilized. Bob reached out for me directly and not only renewed the sponsorship and our leadership coaching, but he expanded both dramatically. I didn't expect that this would happen, and that is not why I was there for Bob when things were particularly rough. I don't know, maybe it is a Karma thing, but to have meaningful business relationships we must be there for each other especially in challenging times.

Politely decline some business opportunities... even if it costs your firm revenue

A while back, a long-time client of Stand & Deliver reached out for Mary and me to say they wanted to start a seminar series dealing with a particular topic involving a specific group of their executives. Mary and

I talked about it and agreed that not only were we not the right firm to do this, but that attempting to do the seminar series was potentially problematic for our client. There was real revenue involved paying us for our leadership seminar services, but we genuinely felt that it didn't make sense. It wasn't strategic or practical. Mary and I believe strongly that turning down the business in this case and explaining the way we did only strengthened our relationship with this client and the leaders of the firm. As I said in this chapter, "sales" isn't the same as meaningful strategic relationships building. Sometimes turning down the business is just the right thing to do.

Own your mistakes...no excuses!

One of the most impactful ways to strengthen a business relationship is by simply acknowledging that a mistake was made and that you as the leader of your organization take full responsibility. Too many people in business only make excuses when things go wrong and point the fingers at others doing everything they can to avoid taking any responsibility. I can't think of anything worse for any relationship. One of the keys to building a strong relationship is building trust and one of the keys to building trust is having the other party know that you respect them too much to do anything other than owning your actions and the performance of your team. The next time something goes wrong on a business engagement and you or anyone on your team had any role in it, step up and take responsibility and then do everything you can to "fix it" or offer something else of value.

Saying "Congratulations" Goes a Long Way

Ever notice how often people in your business universe post an item on social media having to do with a really terrific event that has happened in their professional or personal life? Graduations, marriage, awards, a new home, recognition, etc. Many of us have gone down the Facebook or Instagram "rabbit hole" of just scrolling mindlessly. I know, I'm guilty. However, if you strategically and intentionally look at social media to see opportunities to like a post or post a comment saying, "Congrats, well done" or "That's awesome" with a thumbs up or an applause emoji, it's simple and powerful. People appreciate it. Better yet, send a text or an e-mail of congratulations to a business stakeholder that just had something great happen in his or her life. And I know it sounds old school, but I've picked up the phone and called someone to congratulate him or her. Even if you have to leave a message, it makes a difference; it makes people feel good and strengthens that relationship.

Never stop saying "Thank You"

So many of us in the world of business work so hard to secure a deal, an engagement, a sponsorship or whatever. Often it involved intense negotiation, compromise, getting into the weeds of an agreement. And all too often, once the deal does get done, too many leaders take it for granted and then it is "next." But real relationships building often involves simply saying "thank you". It doesn't sound like a big deal, but it is. We are all moving so fast on the treadmill of life that we don't stop long enough to acknowledge others. It's not only a mistake, but it is also disrespectful to key stakeholders. Get in the habit of saying thanks more—and mean it, because it matters.

Doing everything "right" doesn't guarantee success.

This hub and spokes strategic business relationship building philosophy is no guarantee that a relationship you want or believe you should have will play out that way. Let me give you an example. Mary and I have worked with a particular client for over a decade. The company sponsored our programming, and we led a Leadership Academy there as well. The CEO constantly told us how thrilled he was with the service we provided. We were always there for him, consistently doing things and providing services outside of our business engagement. There were tons of calls during off hours, listening to his issues and offering advice and consultation—at no cost. We did it because it was the right thing to do. We did it to be helpful and of service. And then something really odd happened.

When the pandemic hit and COVID became all too real in March 2020, we knew that the world would never be the same and our business relationships would be greatly affected no matter how hard we tried.

Mary and I reached out consistently to our business stakeholders offering to be helpful. But in this particular situation described above, this company's CEO went radio silent. Months later, it was clear to us that the company's revenue picture had improved significantly, and they were back on their feet. We would have loved to have done business with them again, but the CEO in question not only didn't reach out to us, but when I e-mailed, texted and left a voicemail for him saying we should talk, there was no response.

See, here's the thing. Having a strong business relationship doesn't always mean that it's going to translate into more business for your company. I'm not even talking about that in this case. I incorrectly assumed that he would have the courtesy of simply responding and saying something like, "Listen, Steve, even though our company is back, we are not in a position to sponsor your programming any longer." While disappointed, I would have felt better about the relationship. As Mary often says, "We are all adults." We can handle a "no". We can handle a rejection. In many ways it is the exact opposite of what happened with our friend Bob described earlier. So, here's the point. You can work the hub and spokes strategic relationship building perfectly and certain clients will disappoint you. That's just the way it is sometimes and all of us, myself included, have to work harder to not take it personally (which I would be lying to say I didn't on some level) and realize that is just how some people are.

Be a Trusted Advisor

Meaningful business relationships can't simply be about doing what is "in the agreement." Of course, contractual agreements lay out specific services to be provided and at the bare minimum that is exactly what we should be doing. But if that is all we do, it is often not going to be enough. What I mean is that we must consistently bring value and provide service outside of said agreement. There are numerous business situations where Mary and I provide help including offering advice about succession planning, branding and making ourselves available to participants in our Leadership Academy outside of formal coaching appointments or seminars. We provide everyone our cell phone number and encourage them to reach out, and many of them do. Do we have to manage this approach so it doesn't get out of control? Of course. While most stakeholders don't abuse it, they do appreciate it, although not all to the same degree. Simply put, be there—which means being accessible and available to offer not just an attentive ear, but also your ability to listen and offer the best advice and feedback if asked.

Chapter 12
Strategic Leadership and Communication: "Connecting the Dots"

Strategic leadership? How does a leader communicate in a strategic fashion? What exactly does it mean to be a strategic leader? For me, it comes down to asking some key questions of yourself as a leader who must connect and engage with a complex set of stakeholders and audiences.

What are some of these questions? Why did a particular leader do what he did? What was his rationale? What was he or she trying to accomplish? Did that leader even need to pursue a particular goal and were there other options to consider? Or, what about the leader who makes a presentation at a meeting with others wondering; "What exactly is her point?" Or is she simply talking because she has a slot on a meeting agenda and is required to speak?

Too often, we as leaders do and say things that have no strategic rationale. It's like we are on "auto-pilot"—going through the motions. But being a strategic leader requires that we slow down...actually *think*... and ask ourselves; "What exactly *is* my goal?" What specifically am I trying to accomplish and what is the best way to communicate with a particular audience to help move and motivate them in that direction? We must also recognize trends, challenges and opportunities and think through the best ways to adapt, pivot and respond to unexpected disruption—think COVID-19 and global pandemic.

"Connecting the Dots"

I often talk to Mary about the need to "connect the dots." It sounds so simple—you know, see how a particular trend, situation or event is "connected" to another and lead accordingly. Yet, many leaders not only don't connect the dots, but they also don't even realize there are dots to be connected in the first place.

Consider if the so-called leaders at Blockbuster had "connected the dots," they would not have so cavalierly rejected the offer in 2000 to acquire Netflix. In fact, the CEO of Blockbuster at the time actually scoffed at the prospect—convinced that Blockbuster's market status was rock solid. If newspapers had "connected the dots" they may have expanded and diversified to "digital" video content well before others captured much of that market opportunity and consumer demand. For many leaders, they believe their job is to simply "deal with the situation" at a particular time without connecting the dots as to where trends and market forces are likely to go. This linear leadership approach is often a dangerous mistake. As hockey great Wayne Gretzky famously once said, "I skate to where the puck is going to be, not to where it has been."

I've come to realize, however, that connecting the dots is not natural for many professionals. At the risk of sounding like a leadership know-it-all (trust me, nobody is) it's clear that connecting the dots requires a lot of thought and a very strategic and innovative mindset. But strategic thinking, leadership and communication also demand your attention, time and a deep commitment to do more than what your job description states as a CEO, COO or whatever your title may be. It means you must care deeply to help put your team or organization in a position to grow, evolve and succeed. Simply put, this type of strategic leadership and "connecting the dots" is not easy—but it can be learned. Yet, those who either can't, or won't, attempt to learn this put themselves and their organization in a highly vulnerable position. Opportunities are missed. Key decisions are not made. The proverbial train passes them by. These leaders often think in a more linear fashion as if they have the luxury of moving from A to B and then to C, etc. This simplistic and flawed leadership approach just won't cut it in a highly competitive, fluid and constantly evolving environment. As I've previously stated, these linear leaders sometimes don't even know that there are "dots" that need to be connected. These dots are a combination of data points, trends, occurrences, events, etc. Think about those in high profile, highly public positions that need to make decisions on the fly. They must be adept at thinking ahead—and what effect their words and actions will have. Consider Chesley "Sully" Sullenberger, who successfully and safely landed a US Airways plane in the Hudson River in January 2009. He could have panicked. He could have frozen. But he didn't. He thought clearly, strategically, and quickly, considering his options and ultimately deciding on what he believed to be the best decision and then executed along with his team members. He was calm, clear, and focused and he saved a lot of lives. If this isn't strategic and exceptional leadership, then I don't know what is.

Presidential Leadership Requires Strategic Thinking

Consider some additional examples involving leaders whose leadership we all greatly rely on. I respect President Joe Biden, but there are times it seems that he is just not the strategic leader he needs to be. Consider that in an interview with ABC News in late 2021, President Biden was asked why his administration seemed so ill-prepared to provide the massive and appropriate amount of testing required (either at home or in places across the country) when the Omicron variant exploded before Thanksgiving of that year. The President's response was revealing on many levels when he implied nobody saw it coming.

That's just not true. For well over a year scientists and health experts were consistently saying that the COVID virus would mutate and that we could likely expect new variants in the future. Biden and his public health team didn't know it was going to be called Omicron, but it is simply not true that this new variant hit our nation out of the blue. The President and his team did not strategically think, lead and manage by making the right decisions at the right time to prepare to have an appropriate number of tests ready instead of having millions of Americans scrambling to find a test at home or standing in line for hours, often in the cold, at a government run testing site. As a leader, President Biden and his team simply didn't "connect the dots" and these dots were not that hard to connect. A remotely strategic leader would have seen it coming.

I hate to pile on President Biden, who seems to genuinely care about helping others, but a very similar thing happened involving the withdrawal of American troops in Afghanistan. He and his military team knew that American troops were going to withdraw from a nation we had been at war with for 2-decades since 9/11. Everyone knew it. Clearly, the withdrawal of American troops was not going to be easy. It was going to be complicated and dangerous. President Biden and his team also knew that there were many Afghanis who worked and fought shoulder to shoulder with American troops battling the Taliban. President Biden knew that there had to be a thoughtful, strategic and practical plan to withdraw not only American troops but other Afghani-American allies out of a country in chaos. That just didn't happen. You don't need me to remind you of heartbreaking pictures of the violence, confusion and tragedy that happened in those fateful days at the Kabul airport. And when confronted with this leadership failure, President Biden said in numerous public forums that no one could have predicted this was going to happen. Again, just not true.

Being Strategic Requires Being Calm and Decisive

In such high-pressured, sensitive, and potentially dangerous situations, strategic leadership is more important than ever. To be clear, I am not saying you can predict with certainty exactly how things are going to play out, because a lot of things do just happen and being a strategic leader doesn't mean you can realistically prepare for every potential event, outcome or scenario. However, the best, most thoughtful, strategic leaders must have the ability to calmly and decisively consider a variety of options as to how an organization should respond— especially when the pressure is on. Strategic leaders can't predict or anticipate the future, but they must understand that "the status quo is rarely if ever an option" (unless doing nothing and not acting is in fact the best option available to you at that time) and that "change is the only constant." One of the greatest leadership attributes is in fact the ability to think on one's feet.

These are not empty leadership mottos or cliches, but rather must be ingrained into a leader's DNA. This is "tough stuff" because all of us at some point have said to ourselves—especially when things are going well and the team is "winning"—"If things could only stay the way they are..." Well, the best, most strategic leaders understand that there is no such thing as things staying the way they are. Strategic leaders anticipate change. They expect disruptions. Sometimes big disruptions. They are prepared to adapt, adjust and pivot with both a sense of urgency and yet with a sense of calm and strategic perspective. I know this is easier said than done. I know that I have significant leadership shortcomings, yet, I have come to realize that one of my positive attributes is that I am a pretty good strategic leader, especially when these so-called "unexpected things" happen. (This is after I learned to better manage my emotions and not seek to blame so quickly when things go wrong.)

Leadership Lessons from My Father: A Newark Visionary

In many ways, it is a leadership approach that has been developed in large part due to how I grew up and who I grew up around. More specifically, my late father, Steve Adubato, Sr., who I wrote candidly about in, *Lessons in Leadership*, taught me an awful lot about leading in this very strategic fashion—even if he had no formal name for it. It was my father's ability to think and lead in a very strategic and forward-thinking fashion that somehow became ingrained into my leadership DNA. This "connecting the dots" mindset is something I developed over time, but it started with observing my father. A lot of what I saw in my father in the early 1970s was a leadership mindset involving anticipating some significant disruption or change in the "universe" he was operating in.

While I explored my father's sometimes less than tactful way of dealing with people, it was his ability to see possibilities others never imagined that was exceptional. He was a true visionary. A couple of examples: in the late 60s and early 70s in the city of Newark, NJ where we lived, there was a significant shift in the city's demographics. Simply put, many of our white neighbors were moving out and Newark was becoming more black and brown. My father had been active in Newark politics and was looking to start a non-profit organization that would serve the needs of our community. So, against the popular opinion in our largely Italian-American "neighborhood," my father decided to actively support underdog Ken Gibson for mayor. Gibson would not only become the first black mayor of Newark, but also the first black mayor on the eastern seaboard. My father liked and respected Gibson—plus the other two white candidates for mayor included an incumbent who was later sent to jail for his dealings with the mob and another local white vigilante who my father never saw eye to eye with. It was clear to my father that Ken Gibson was the best option for the city to move forward. But to be clear, doing this was also tremendously risky and dangerous, not just politically, but on a very personal safety level to my father and our family. (I wrote about this extensively in *Lessons in Leadership*.)

The point here is that my father realized that things were changing in Newark. The population was shifting dramatically, and if he was to create a community-based non-profit organization, which in fact became The North Ward Center in 1970, he would need the active support and municipal funding from the new mayor. So, my father forged an important and historical relationship with Mayor Ken Gibson. In part that relationship helped grow the North Ward Center into one of the most significant social services organizations in the country and it also helped thousands of residents in our community. Strategic and forward-thinking leadership. Again, this was very "tough stuff", but it was also required to move forward in a productive fashion.

Later, the other strategic and forward-thinking leadership demonstrated by my father, who was a long-time public-school teacher before leaving out of frustration after many years, involved education. My father was convinced that the public schools in Newark were not adequately serving the educational needs of the children in the city. So, instead of simply complaining about it, he used his political influence, relationships and vision to create the first charter school in the city. The Robert Treat Academy was founded in 1997 and was named after the original founder of Newark, Robert Treat. Over the years, the Robert Treat Academy has positively impacted the lives of thousands of Newark children, largely because the standard for teaching and student-excellence was established by my father and carried out by the able leaders of that organization.

Why does this all matter? It matters because for certain leaders, in this case my father, Steve Adubato, Sr., being strategic meant not just looking at where things are at a certain point in time, but having the vision, imagination and courage necessary to understand future trends and create a new and better reality. That's what my father did in supporting Ken Gibson for mayor, in creating The North Ward Center and in establishing and building the Robert Treat Academy Charter School. Those things just didn't happen; they were in fact dots that my father saw and then connected, which is what the most exceptional strategic and visionary leaders do.

Chapter 13
The Best Leaders Can Connect
on Any Playing Field

I know you'd rather be communicating and connecting in person... me too. But sometimes, that is simply not possible or even preferable for a variety of reasons. Great leaders must be able to connect with any audience—regardless of the platform. Clearly, in person communication in most settings is preferable. I love when I am able to present to and engage with an audience that is right in front of me, versus an audience in which we interact on a computer screen as if we are a modern-day version of "The Brady Bunch" in a series of "boxes" in "gallery view" on Zoom or whatever platform you are using. (Not to mention that every digital device has a different set up and format.)

As I write this chapter, the ebb and flow of COVID continues. We are about 2-years plus into this global pandemic. Things calm down and we do some things more in person, and then the next day, we are told there is a "new variant" that changes the world around us and we return to a remote setting, constantly pivoting and adapting. It's what we as leaders do.

Yet, I've come to the conclusion that regardless of the state of COVID, the need for leaders to effectively communicate in a remote setting is a skill and competency that is going to be required moving forward. The decisions around how we engage each other, be it in person or remotely, will be dictated more and more by issues involving logistics, travel, economics and people's individual preference. Weather emergencies, natural disasters and other catastrophic events also dictate this need to adapt to remote communication. I believe that many of us as leaders—myself included—fell short of being forward thinking, strategic and innovative enough in this area well before COVID hit us in March 2020. I admit it; our team was caught off guard and we were unprepared to move smoothly by pivoting to lead, communicate and engage on a remote digital platform. This leadership shortcoming falls on me as our unofficial "chief strategy officer." Some might argue this is an unrealistic leadership standard, but if we are talking about the best, most innovative and strategic leaders who understand the need to prepare for what many consider to be "unexpected" circumstances or major shifts in our business universe, it is incumbent upon us to rise to this standard.

But we can't go back. There are no "mulligans" when it comes to leading, especially when it comes to "the tough stuff." So, now that we know that the need to communicate and connect in a remote world is an essential leadership requirement, let's consider some practical tips and tools in this area:

—**Find the camera.** Two years plus into this pandemic as I write this chapter, I am struck by how many leaders at every level of all kinds of organizations can't find the camera on their digital device. They are looking all over the place and when I've coached and challenged some of them to communicate into the camera, they often say it is "unnatural" or "just doesn't feel right." Some will tell me they like to "look at others on the screen" because it feels more like they are talking directly to their audience. But there is an obvious problem with this approach, because the ONLY way to connect with your audience is not by looking at them on your screen, but rather by looking directly into the camera. That is how others see you looking at them making "eye contact." Until the technology changes, I don't know of any other way to "make the connection with others." I know it's difficult. I know it's unnatural. As I often say in my leadership seminars and my executive coaching, I don't make the rules; I am just pretty sure I know what they are. So, step 1, find the camera.

—**Practice makes progress.** Given that communicating into a green or red dot on your device, (which is in fact your camera), is not easy, let's acknowledge that this takes practice. You must consistently, patiently and persistently work at looking into the camera and talking as well as listening. Can you glance occasionally at others on the screen? Of course, but do not engage in sustained interaction with them because simply put, to your audience, it looks like you are disengaged. I argue that in every interaction—even the most informal and casual one—looking into the camera and communicating is an essential leadership tool. The more you do it the more natural and less unnatural it becomes. No, it will never be normal, but since it is required, the best leaders must at least be competent in this area.

—**Don't assume your internet connection is working.** Sounds crazy, right? But Mary and I have led so many seminars in which leaders are presenting or communicating and because they sound fine to themselves, they assume that others in that meeting are hearing and seeing them in the same way. With often-shaky internet connections, we can't assume that. So, what do we do? My advice? Any time you are communicating, presenting or engaging others in a remote setting, make it clear up front that any time there is any part of your presentation that is not coming across or being easily understood, ask them to simply call a time out (yes, politely interrupt you) and ask you to repeat what you've said. And, yes, there are times that if the internet connection is so poor that you have to log out and log back in to try to get a better connection. Consider using a hardwired connection rather than wifi. It often proves more stable and reliable. Finally, if for whatever reason or reasons that connection doesn't work, I say reschedule if you can't move to another location with a stronger internet connection.

—**Audio only…really?** That won't work. As long as we've been in this global pandemic, there are still meetings that take place in which certain team members either refuse to or just say, "I don't like being on video." That's just not okay. Early on in 2020, it is understandable that people needed to adapt, adjust and find a location in which they could participate remotely. But after a reasonable amount of time, there really is no credible reason for people to say they only want to be on audio. You wouldn't be able to do that if you were meeting in person. You can't say, "I'm just going to stand out in the hallway where no one can see me and every once in a while I will yell into the meeting with my thoughts and feedback." Obviously this would be unprofessional and unacceptable. So, get dressed. I'm not talking suit and tie for every meeting but be presentable. Get yourself together because it is called "work", not play time. Have I been more casual (okay, I have worn my Yankees hoodie) for certain online interactions? Yes, especially with our internal team members. But you must know your audience and the context of the interaction and dress appropriately. This includes being seen as well as being heard. We all know that when people are "audio only" for a remote meeting, they are less engaged and more tempted to be distracted by other devices—especially a cell phone—checking, and at times responding to, text messages and e-mails. It is hard enough connecting and engaging remotely, but if you are not seen as well as heard, in some cases you might as well not do it at all.

—**Be more concise and clear.** Let's accept it. In remote communication, many leaders and team members are distracted. Our attention span is shorter. We wander. So, get to the point faster. Lead shorter meetings. Don't drone on. If you have a 5- or 6-minute presentation that you've planned, turn it into a 3-minute presentation. Edit yourself. Cut out a lot of detail. Much of it will be forgotten anyway. We need to accept the reality that people are in too many remote meetings and many leaders complain of being "Zoomed out," so if you are going to have such a meeting or deliver a presentation, just get to your main point...a lot faster!

—**Engage them.** In my chapter in this book on "forced engagement," I talked extensively about this. But simply put, in a remote setting, people MUST be engaged. The longer you hear one person's voice in a remote setting, the more likely your audience is to become disengaged and disconnected. Get others talking. Ask more open-ended questions of individual team members. This takes practice, persistence and assertiveness, but engaging others pays off big time in the remote world.

—**Cut down or eliminate your PowerPoint.** That's right; only use it if you must. Only use it if it adds a lot to your oral presentation. Realize that as soon as you opt to use PowerPoint, you minimize the screen of participants. The PowerPoint takes over, and the meeting participants are usually in a narrow column along the righthand side of your screen. We are not even talking about all of them, but just how many will fit there. You can't see them, and many will not be able to see you. Your PowerPoint slide often becomes another barrier between you and your audience and the last thing you need when communicating remotely versus in person is another barrier. Further, if you do use PowerPoint to support your message, take it down and go back to the "gallery view" quickly. Don't let the PowerPoint sit there and dominate your interaction. It is not necessary and only complicates your remote communication.

—**Get your lighting right.** I'm no lighting expert, and after all this time I am still experimenting in this area. In fact, just last week I had light shooting in from a window on my right in our home library I started using for Zoom meetings. Together with Mary, we figured out a very high-tech solution to the problem. What did we do? Taped dark cardboard to cover the window until Mary (on the other end of a remote rehearsal) said the light vector coming from the window onto my head was no longer there. Sure, my wife Jennifer says we are waiting on some room darkening shades for this window, but the "supply chain" is delaying it. (Where have I heard that before?) So, for now, it's cardboard in the window, but the point is, you have to get your lighting right so you are seen in a favorable light.

—**Simplify your background.** Just today as I am writing this chapter from the library in our home, I asked Mary about my background and while she thought it looked okay, she said it was a bit too busy, so we took some items down. As communicators, the goal is to have an attractive background but one that does not distract or detract from you. All of our public broadcasting programming is now produced in a home studio with a simple blue background. Mary has a comparable background as she co-hosts our podcast, "Lessons in Leadership." But before we simplified our backgrounds, we had lots of pictures and knickknacks behind each of us. That may be fine for our family Zoom meetings, but in a professional setting, a simple, clean background is always better.

—**Lean in.** Yes, that's right, get closer to the camera. Fill up your screen, especially when presenting. I'm not talking about sticking your face just inches from the camera, but when people hang back or lean back in their chair, they become smaller and less significant. It takes away from their message and their executive presence. You wouldn't sit back in in your chair in an in-person presentation. Rather, you would lean in. Lean forward. You must do the same in a remote setting, which takes practice and self-awareness. It is essential to connecting with your audience, especially when you are attempting to persuade your audience and motivate them to act.

—**Bring your passion.** I'm convinced that in order to connect remotely, people need to not just see, but feel, how strongly you believe what you are saying. That takes passion and, yes, energy. No, I'm not talking about screaming or yelling or using out of control hand gestures, but your audience needs to know that you are "into this" and sometimes that takes you tapping into your passion, because your audience needs to feel passionately as well. Low key, remote communication has its place particularly when dealing with sensitive or difficult issues, but when you are engaging and trying to persuade your audience in a remote setting, a lack of passion can be deadly.

—**Please...don't read.** I know you have a script. I know you have lots of information you want to make sure you get across. But as soon as you start reading, your eyes will be looking away from the camera, which means away from your audience, and no matter how good you are at "reading," your audience will feel disconnected. Get rid of your script. Turn that script into a few key bullet points that allow you to stay focused, but also to be "conversational." Mary and I call it "filling in the white space" in between those bullets. The more conversational you are—especially looking into the camera—the more likely you are to connect with your audience. You can't do that if you are reading your script.

—**Be present.** Eliminate your distractions. If we are being really honest, virtually all of us will admit that in a remote meeting we have on occasion checked e-mail and text messages. I'm guilty, but I've also come to realize that especially when the stakes are high in a remote meeting, the need to be more present and focused is more critical than ever. If you are on a computer, take your iPhone and put it to the side, on vibrate or turn it upside down. People can tell when you are multitasking in remote format. And even if they don't, your multitasking will cause you to miss something—potentially something important. So...don't do it. It will send the message that you are distracted and the meeting you are in just isn't that important, which means that your audience is not that important. That may not be your intent, but that is the effect. Limit distractions and be more present.

—**Remember...you are always "on."** There are too many embarrassing examples where prominent leaders on Zoom have been caught doing inappropriate things or were dressed in pajamas or yes, underwear, because somehow, they convinced themselves that they weren't "on" and seen by others in the meeting and in the social media "afterlife." So just assume you are "on" until you shut your laptop down and then go about your business.

—**Slow down.** I talked earlier in this chapter about the need to be concise and clear. About the need to get to the point faster. Please don't confuse this with fast talking. Because you are in a remote setting and not in person, sometimes it is harder to understand exactly what you are saying. So, pausing and using deliberate enunciated communication is critical to have the message sent be the message received. Fast talkers who often sound as if they are mumbling or jumbling words together can give off the impression that they are either nervous or are frankly not that concerned about others understanding them, which is not what the best leaders are shooting for. Be aware that some communication platforms also convert speech to text. This form of Artificial Intelligence is not perfect, and words jumbled together will be hard to translate into accurate text.

—**Listen...really listen.** I wrote about this in "Lessons in Leadership" when focusing on how hard active, engaged listening really is. But if its challenging in person, imagine how much more difficult it is in a remote setting. Fight the urge to interrupt too often. If you must interrupt, do it strategically by seeking clarification or attempting to engage others. ("I'm sorry for interrupting, but I just want to ask you...") But impatient leaders who don't let others finish their thoughts in a remote setting can often cause other team members and stakeholders to shut down. I must constantly work to be a better listener because I know I am too impatient and too quick to want to get to the "bottom line." This desire to communicate and lead with a sense of urgency must be balanced with the need to have others feel heard and appreciated and being a better, more engaged, listener will go a long way in that regard.

—**Show up early and check your technology.** I'm sure Mary is laughing as we write this chapter together because this is one of my greatest leadership shortcomings. I have some unhealthy, unresolved habit of jumping into a remote meeting at the last minute, Inevitably, there are technological issues that of course I call Mary to help resolve. But if I had checked in 5-minutes earlier, it would give us more time to get the kinks out and get ourselves focused. While I am working on this, I haven't made enough progress. So don't be like me. Show up early, check in, check your shot, your lighting, your internet, your audio and get confirmation from a trusted team member that you are ready to go.

—**Do a post-remote game recap.** Just like the best sports teams do, have a brief discussion after the remote meeting or forum as to what went well, what went wrong, what needs to be improved, what lessons were learned and what exactly will be done in your next remote interaction that will help you and your team improve.

Chapter 14

Don't Sweat the Q&A

I'm fascinated by how many professionals in positions of leadership communicate poorly and panic when they face challenging questions regarding what has happened, what they have proposed or whether they did or did not do something. I am talking about answering questions under pressure in a challenging situation in which your audience is curious and, in some cases, concerned as to what you've presented. They want to better understand and know more. They want clarification and reassurance, and it is your job as a leader to seize this Q&A opportunity and make the most of it.

In 2008, I dedicated an entire book, entitled *What Were They Thinking? Crisis Communication: The Good, the Bad and the Totally Clueless,* to this type of communication. That book was about "crisis communication," while in this chapter I am largely referring to the challenging questions directed to a leader who has made a presentation to an audience that must "buy in" to what has been proposed. I've come to realize that many leaders struggle mightily in this area, largely due to how they perceive the Q&A experience. Once again, much of this leadership and communication competency comes down to one's mindset, which greatly impacts a leader's performance. Consider that many of my coaching clients have shared the following comments regarding the "Q&A" after they have made a presentation:

"I get so stressed out after I deliver a presentation before the board. What if I am asked a question and I don't have the answer?"

"What if I blank out and lose my train of thought?"

"Sometimes I think the person asking the question has an ulterior motive."

To the untrained and uncoached leader, this list of concerns is understandable. It also implies an unhealthy and, yes, unproductive, attitude and approach to the Q&A.

Here is how I see the "Q&A." Virtually every one of these "what ifs" expressed by leaders I have coached (as well as many reading this right now) is unwarranted. Really challenging questions from a somewhat skeptical audience actually present an excellent opportunity to engage and connect with your audience. Challenging questions allow a leader to clarify his or her message. They also give a presenter a unique opportunity to better identify and understand the potential opposition or resistance key stakeholders may have to what you have proposed or the position you've taken.

Think about it. Many leaders say they don't want to be asked tough questions. But what if this so called "tough question" is on the mind of someone in your audience who could have a significant impact on implementing your idea, initiative, or proposal? Why would a leader NOT want to know what is on the mind of his or her audience? Wouldn't you want the opportunity to take that tough question head-on and, in turn, respond to any potential opposition or confusion? If such a question isn't asked that is still on the mind of certain audience members that you need to persuade, then the leader has a real, more difficult problem. Why? Because the opposition and concerns still exist, but they haven't been publicly stated and put out in the open. Rather, that opposition and those nagging concerns are talked about in private (behind your back) which doesn't allow you to respond in a strategic, assertive, and thoughtful fashion. Experience tells me that challenging and difficult questions must be seen in a more constructive and positive light if a leader is to motivate and inspire key stakeholders to act or move in a particular direction.

With this more positive, opportunistic communication approach in mind to the Q&A, consider the following tips and tools that will help any leader remain confident and composed when dealing with challenging questions after (or during) your presentation.

—**Be patient and listen to the entire question.** Pause—take a moment to think through the entire question before you respond. Listen to understand versus listening to simply respond. Too many of us are so anxious to let the questioner know that we have an "answer" to a question that we jump in too quickly, often cutting off the questioner because in our minds we already "know" what they are asking. Here's the problem with this approach. First, it disrespects the questioner, and it sends the message that you are so anxious to respond that you really don't care that much about hearing the entire question or about the questioner him or herself. It is rude, I know, I've done it when I'm not in "listening mode." And, even if you come up with the so-called "right answer," you have unnecessarily alienated a potentially important stakeholder or decision maker in your audience. Let the questioner get out the entire question and then listen...really listen...and then calmly and confidently respond accordingly.

—**Breathe.** I mean, actually *breathe.* I am not an expert on the biophysics involved in communicating in a situation that creates some degree of pressure and anxiety, but I have coached many leaders who simply forget to breathe under these circumstances. It's actually happened to me in a few, but very memorable, painful experiences. These leaders are so nervous that they border on hyperventilating. Practice slowing down your breathing, cadence and, yes, *pause,* not just to think more clearly but to communicate in a more thoughtful and deliberate fashion.

—**Respond to a challenging question in an assertive and proactive fashion.** For years I have tried to teach and coach our leadership clients to communicate by pivoting or bridging to their main message. Here is what this means. Too many leaders, when asked a challenging question, attempt to respond by simply giving too much detail and responding to the question in what they believe is such a thorough fashion that they get caught "in the weeds." They provide so much detail, so many specifics, and they respond for so long that they not only lose their audience, but it is unclear exactly what their message is.

I propose that when asked a question, a leader respond succinctly and briefly for approximately 15 seconds, and no more than 30, and then "pivot" back to their main message. When I say "pivot," I mean to transition using such phrases as, "what really matters here is..." or "the key message I want to get across is..." or "what I know many in the audience care deeply about is..." By using this more assertive, proactive, and strategic communication approach, a leader can reframe and manage the Q&A in a more impactful fashion. Finally, I am not talking about ducking or ignoring the question, but I am saying that responding to questions in a public forum is not the same as responding to a lawyer's question in a court of law. Pivoting and transitioning back to your main message is appropriate and effective when trying to persuade and move a particular audience, which is not acceptable in a court of law but is appropriate and effective in the court of public opinion.

—**Flip the script.** Instead of waiting to be asked a particularly challenging question, there are certain cases in which you should raise the question yourself. Here is how this works. If a leader is confident that there are specific concerns or opposition to what he or she is proposing, but the question hasn't been asked yet, I say, bring it up yourself. Consider this example; "I'm sure some of you here today are wondering, how are we going to pay for the initiative I am proposing?" Why take this approach? Because there are likely people in your audience that are wondering how you are going to pay for this. See it as an opportunity to respond to potential concerns or opposition by being proactive and assertive. It also communicates how confident you are because you have raised the issue instead of being on the defensive and simply responding. As they say, the best defense is often a good offense.

—**Be concise.** Have you ever noticed in a Q&A a leader can drone on forever? Monitor yourself. Get to your point concisely and quickly. One of the communication techniques I have used in my coaching is to encourage leaders to use the phrase, "so my point is..." Using this phrase is a trigger. It forces you to get to the point. Some leaders are so unaware of how long they have been talking (and in turn how they have lost their audience) that they pay a hefty and unnecessary price.

—**Stay within the goal posts.** No, I am not actually talking football, but I am talking about the way a leader must communicate in a disciplined and strategic fashion when answering tough questions. I have had many clients (and we've seen many very public leaders) say ridiculous, embarrassing, and off-the-wall things in the so-called Q&A. Why is that?

Because they don't communicate within the goal posts. What's inside the goal posts? Primarily it is some version of your main message. It also gives you a visual representation of how far you should and will go in what you say in public in response to a question. This doesn't happen without significant preparation and strategic thinking before the Q&A. Finally, when a leader does not prepare using this goal posts approach, he or she is likely to communicate so far outside the goal posts that they wind up retracting, clarifying and that they say they "were taken out of context." None of these excuses are acceptable for really strong and prepared leaders dealing with a Q&A.

—**Don't debate a questioner.** I have a question. When was the last debate or argument you won? Me? I can't remember. We don't "win" arguments or debates and in a Q&A you are not likely to win either. "Okay, Steve, but what about if someone asks the question or makes a statement after my presentation that I think is dead wrong?" I say, if your objective is to engage and bring your audience along with you, then you must respect the audience member's question and frankly respond like this; "Jim, I'm curious. Tell me why you see it that way?" Or, "Jane, your question is an important one. Tell me what your greatest concern is?" Or, "I want to better understand, Bob. Do you have a concrete example of what you're describing?" If you start debating or arguing, no matter how good you think your points are, a challenging questioner isn't likely to say; "Wow, Steve. You raised a great point. I am wrong and you are right!" That just doesn't happen. I'm not saying to patronize your audience, but rather appreciate that there are different points of view and perspectives because everyone is different. In turn, a leader must communicate that he or she cares to understand rather than simply convince the audience that they are right. Yes, you must be persuasive, but there are lots of creative ways of going about this.

—**Anticipate the three or four toughest questions you are likely to be asked.** In preparing for the Q&A after your presentation, think about what your audience is likely to be asking. You are not going to get it 100% right, but you will identify and think through certain obvious questions and prepare for how you would respond. When people don't do this, they get thrown off their game. They are stumped. They look confused. They start rambling and that's when they often go far outside the goal posts and say things out of panic or confusion. The more you prepare for the difficult or challenging questions you are likely to be asked, the more confident and composed you will be during the Q&A.

—**Give the questioner credit.** Acknowledge that a particularly insightful question has caused you to revise your proposal or initiative. An audience member may raise a question or issue that you haven't considered. Give them credit, acknowledge it, and consider incorporating the core message in that question or statement into a better and more comprehensive proposal. Again, this is not a competition or a debate. Further, an audience member has the potential to contribute greatly to what you've proposed. This can only happen when a leader has an open mind and a desire to engage and move forward together.

—**Don't be afraid to say, "I don't know."** It is often an unforced error for a leader to act like they know the answer to a question when they clearly don't. One of the worst things a leader can do is to say something dishonest or to make a statement that they can't back up just because they feel the need to "answer the question." I am a firm believer that if a respected member of your audience asks a question that you don't know the answer to and haven't thought about, it is actually the "right answer" to say; "Bob, I actually don't know the answer to that question, but clearly your question matters…" The leader in responding must make it clear to Bob that he will do what is necessary to find out the answer and pursue the issue further. I don't mean simply saying it, but actually doing it and publicly stating how exactly you will follow up and by when and then make sure you get back to Bob. For a leader to say, "I don't know" (occasionally but not too often), communicates a sense of candor and honesty as well as a sense of integrity and character. Finally, it also shows how confident you are by acknowledging that you don't know something and you respect your audience too much to make up an unfounded answer on the spot.

So, the bottom line? The Q&A doesn't have to be so stressful and anxiety producing. Rather, it should be a unique and exciting opportunity for a leader to engage and connect with an audience who has difficult and challenging questions. An audience you need to be on board with you if you and the team are going to move forward together.

Chapter 15
The Wellness-Leadership Connection

I've waited a long time to write the final chapter of this book focused on the connection between wellness and leadership. Fact is, it was less of me "waiting" to write this chapter and more that I really struggled for months to figure out exactly *how* to write it. How was I going to frame this chapter? What message did I want to send and share? And, to what degree was I even qualified to write such a chapter on wellness and leadership?

I've stalled long enough—so I draft these words on the final days of 2022 sitting in my favorite coffee shop in my hometown of Montclair, NJ. It is during the "holiday break" between Christmas and New Year's Day, and I am not stressed by the day-to-day responsibilities of leading our two organizations with my colleague Mary Gamba. It is Friday, December 30, which is significant in itself. For the past several years, I've made Fridays my so-called "wellness day," during which I dedicate the morning to a workout (thanks Peloton) followed by a Pilates class (thanks to Barbara at To Be Pilates) and then stretching at a studio that does nothing but stretch people (thanks to Ashlee at Kika Stretch Studios... it is life changing). The coffee shop is right across the street from the stretching studio, where I set time aside to do a lot of reading, writing, and thinking.

Flex Fridays?

Mary and I decided several years ago to make Fridays a "wellness" day—we call them "flex Fridays"—that we would limit our "regular work" communication. If there is a pressing work-related matter that can't wait until Monday morning, we will talk or text. If a team member needs either one of us, they are free to reach out—but Fridays feel different than the other days of the work week. But what does mine or Mary's Friday schedule have to do with the wellness-leadership connection? Here are Mary's thoughts:

"To be a great leader, we must make time to take care of ourselves. Wellness to me means putting on your own oxygen mask first on a plane, before helping others. My decision to request Fridays off many years ago was directly tied to my wellness. My boys were in elementary and middle school at the time, and I simply did not have enough hours in the day to ensure their needs were being met, especially given the hour each way sitting in traffic up and down the Garden State Parkway to get from my house in Westfield to our offices in Montclair. To put it simply, I was at a tipping point, and something had to give. Initially, my Fridays "off" were spent catching up on e-mails or writing proposals that I did not have time to complete during the week. (Just not having the pressure of the commute or the phone ringing nonstop allowed more time to focus.) After that it was volunteering where needed in my son's classrooms, getting things done in the house and any doctor's visits or other appointments.

Today, with a junior in college and a senior in high school, my boys do not need me as much, but my Friday mornings still consist of work-related items I was unable to complete during the week—but then it is truly time for my wellness, taking a walk with the dog (which I now do every evening as well since post-COVID we continue to work from home) or exercising or cleaning the house. As Steve mentioned, we are always available as needed should any urgent work-related matters arise, but Fridays are a time to catch our breath and check in with our own mental and physical wellbeing and that of our families."

But here is one important thing to remember. It is not just about making wellness a priority on a specific day. It needs to be a priority *every day* for you to lead at your best. Real wellness is about a lot more than a morning workout, Pilates, yoga, or stretching, or sitting at a coffee shop on Friday mornings. It is more than Mary taking a time to walk the dog or get things done around the house. It's about prioritizing your medical care and staying on top of health-related issues before it's too late. (Currently, I'm undergoing a series of diagnostic tests to determine why I am experiencing specific pain, which could be both stressful and anxiety producing.) Yes, preventative medicine. However, wellness is also about acknowledging that I deal with "health anxiety"—which often has me thinking the "worst case scenario" with every ache, pain, lump or bump. Wellbeing for me, and millions of others, is dealing with our own mental health. For me that has meant getting talk therapy, but also getting the proper medication to treat both my anxiety as well as occasional depression. Wellness is also about managing stress, getting enough sleep, and investing in the "relationship bank" with people who matter in our lives. I'm talking family and friends, but it is also about trying to avoid or limit our contact with "toxic people" Yes, preventative medicine. It is also about a semblance of this thing called "work-life integration" and perspective. I don't even use the phrase "work-life balance" because I am not exactly sure what that means. What I do know is that when our "work" consumes the rest of our lives, and we are simply not able to "turn it off," it often can have a very negative impact on our wellness—as well as on our performance.

Yvonne Surowiec, Senior Executive Vice President, Chief People Officer, Valley Bank, (our firm Stand & Deliver has facilitated the Valley Leadership Academy for many years) also refers to it as "work-life integration."

Says Surowiec; "There is a scale in terms of how wellness works. It is different for everyone. It is not one size fits all. What's important to one individual may be different for somebody else who has different obligations or who is in a different place from a family perspective. I personally have always incorporated exercise in my own routine, and I've done that intentionally because it helps me be stronger at what I do. It's proven that exercise releases stress...For me, exercise just frees up that other noise and all of a sudden, I'll have this solution to a problem that I haven't been able to figure out for weeks."

Clearly, wellness and leadership involves a strategic, comprehensive and consistent approach to self-care. It is about limiting "screen time" (I'm pretty bad when it comes to sometimes going down the black hole of social media and the Internet). Our wellness and the connection to how we lead is also about our mental health and getting the help we need in this area as opposed to thinking we can always "tough it out" in any situation. That's right, I am talking therapy. I've been there and, when needed, I still go there, because sometimes wellness (and leadership) is about knowing that we can't simply handle it all ourselves and we need help from others who are experts at certain things that we are not.

Consider the perspective of Dr. Amy Frieman, the long-time Chief Wellness Officer, Hackensack Meridian *Health* (HMH), where Mary and I have led the HMH Physician Leadership Academy for many years. Says Dr. Frieman, "Wellness is spiritual. It's physical. It's social. It is emotional. There are a lot of different pieces to well-being. When we talk about the clinician experience, we know that in order to really have high performing clinicians, and to know that they are going to be providing the highest quality patient care, we must have a positive, productive, work-place environment for them. Without that, we will never truly achieve the highest level of well-being."

But for many leaders who are also parents, our wellness is very much tied to the wellbeing of our children. No matter how successful we may be professionally, if one or more of our children, no matter how old they are (as I know firsthand with a daughter who is 12, sons who are 18 and 20 and a son from my first marriage who is 30) is struggling or dealing with a difficult or stressful situation, then not much else seems to matter in our lives. Truth be told, as I am writing this chapter at this particular moment (listening to James Taylor in my Air Pods) my wife Jennifer called, very stressed about a situation involving one of our children. The irony is not lost on me. "Wellness Fridays" are often interrupted by life!

Our Wellness as Leaders Matters...A Lot

So, look, I'm no expert on wellness and too often I know what is best intellectually for my own wellbeing, but I do the exact opposite. For example, wellness is also about staying calm no matter what situation or circumstance we face as leaders. Here's the deal. I try to stay calm (there is a meditation app called CALM that I've tried several times but find myself thinking about my "to do" list and still lose my cool too often. I'm not proud of it and make no excuses.) But I do know from personal experience and coaching hundreds of leaders in every professional field for over two decades that to be a truly effective leader, we have a very real responsibility to focus as much as possible on our wellness. Our wellness directly impacts our performance as leaders. It impacts our ability to make clear-headed decisions on behalf of our organization. It impacts how we respond and react to things that go wrong on our team. It impacts our energy levels as the day goes on and it impacts our ability to be present leaders who are genuinely connected with our team members and committed to their own wellness. When we are off balance and failed to address a wellness issue, it can have a cascading effect.

When it comes to the wellness-leadership connection, as leaders, we have a responsibility to create an organization / team culture that promotes the wellbeing of every team member. It's tough enough to focus on our own wellness, but the best leaders understand that while we can't ensure the wellness of every colleague on our team, we can do things and make decisions that help our teammates prioritize their wellbeing. Some of the actions a great leader can take to promote a "culture of wellness" in the organization or team they are responsible for include the following:

Flextime. Yes, flextime is about the wellness of every team member. While not possible in every organization, particularly those who work on tight deadlines and deliverables, for many of us as leaders, we need to be focused more on the impact of people's work versus the activity of making sure they are "working" a specific set of hours that is rigidly set in stone. Mary calls it "impact over activity." COVID has changed everything, including our need to be more flexible as leaders who prioritize what gets done as opposed to how or when it gets done by those who report to us. Also, organizations can consider early Fridays between Memorial Day and Labor Day or shutting down the week between Christmas and New Year's. Many European companies enjoy this practice.

If possible...work remotely. Allow team members to work remotely when they can "get their work done" effectively and efficiently without having to commute or deal with traffic (New Jersey roads are the worst). Again, Mary spent one hour each way in traffic...on a good day. Just requiring people to come into the office for the sake of coming in is counterproductive, not to mention there are some downsides to physically being in the office which include distractions, lack of focus, or being pulled in different directions.

Reduce the number and length of your meetings. I've been obsessed in the last few years with the "meeting culture" of organizations. There are coaching clients who I am meeting with remotely at 4 in the afternoon who tell me this is their "10th meeting of the day"—which is normal in many organizations. That's insane. That makes no sense. As leaders, we need to stop calling so many meetings that go on forever, and that are debilitating as well as exhausting for team members. You want to do something as a leader to promote a culture of wellness on your team? Look at every meeting you are calling and ask yourself is this meeting necessary and is there is a simpler, less time-consuming way to achieve your objective? I have two small plaques in my office on this topic. One says, "I survived another meeting that should have been an e-mail!" The other one is even more blunt; "This meeting is bullshit!"

Family first. Make "family first" not just a slogan or a catch phrase; make it real. If team members need to deal with their own wellbeing or the wellbeing of family members, it is family first. If a team member is struggling with a family or personal issue, back off and make sure that team member knows that as a leader you understand that the priority in his or her life must always be to their family. Text or call that team member to let them know you are thinking about them. Let them know that you know what is really important. Of course, there are some people who take advantage, but we can't lead and manage based on those exceptions, but rather we need to be empathetic and compassionate leaders who understand that it is not just our family that comes first, it is every team member's as well.

Set time to exercise. This clearly means different things to different people as physical abilities and limitation to exercise are highly personal. For me, I know that if I don't work out early in the morning, I can be cranky the rest of the day. I feel sluggish and just a bit off and I don't have the discipline to "get it done later." For others, they would rather exercise at night and by exercise, I mean anything from a vigorous run or bike ride or walking around the block, stretching, yoga, etc.

Consistently recognize team members for a "job well done." Some might ask what this has to do with promoting a culture of wellness? Simply put, Abraham Maslow made it clear when describing his view on the "Hierarchy of Needs" that all individuals have, that being recognized and acknowledged is pretty important. Knowing that you are appreciated by the leader of your team feels good. Obviously, some team members more than others. Mary consistently makes it clear she would rather get paid more than me thanking her for a job well done. (No joke!) However, most other team members do appreciate it whether they say so or not. As leaders, we must get in the habit of sending an e-mail, text message or calling on the phone and saying in front of other team members that a specific team member has stepped up and done an excellent job.

Check in with team members. Make sure that you do ask how a team member is doing and how you as a leader can be helpful without stepping over the line into someone's personal privacy. Showing that you care is not a leadership technique. It is a way of being. Either you care or you don't, but if you do, show it. If you want the best from your team members, your caring will make a difference to them. Check in with team members on a regular basis because expecting that they will proactively come to you and tell you how they are doing just isn't realistic.

Conduct a Wellness "Self-Assessment." Call a time out...Stop... Think. Take a deep breath and conduct the following wellness self-assessment / mini-survey and encourage each team member to do the same:

> What am I specifically doing to promote my own wellness? (Be specific. Name the top 2 to 3 actions, items and/or activities. Some practical examples include

walking your dog, taking a yoga class, meditating, getting more sleep, reading a chapter in a book or spending more time with your family being truly "present.")

What can and will I do over the next 3-6 months (name one specific action) to improve my well-being, which will in turn help me to be a more focused and effective leader?

At the end of that 3-6 months, how exactly will I assess my progress and incorporate these wellness "tools" into my leadership toolkit?

Manage expectations of team members. I have a habit of sending "weekend e-mails" (much of our programming on public television is broadcast on weekends) regarding particular initiatives, loose ends, items to be followed up on, etc. I'm sure for some team members, this can be irritating and/or disruptive. However, in those e-mails I make it clear that unless there is an emergency that requires immediate attention, then following up and responding to my weekend e-mail on Monday morning is fine. Why is this important? Much of wellness has to do with managing one's stress, and as leaders we can either minimize unhealthy and unnecessary stress or increase it by not being thoughtful and strategic in how we communicate. Trust me, I've done both, but Mary's very candid feedback over the years has changed my approach in this regard.

Let it go. As a leader, I have the habit of sometimes not simply saying what needs to be done without harping on what went wrong, why it went wrong, who did what, etc. Yes, the "blame game." Mary has made it clear that not letting it go after the message has been sent is not only counterproductive, but once again only adds to unnecessary stress, frustration, and an environment that does not support a culture of wellness among team members.

So, here's the deal. As leaders, I strongly believe that we have a basic responsibility to do all we can to prioritize our own wellbeing (obviously certain health and medical issues are beyond anyone's control) as well as the wellbeing of every team member. I wish it were as simple as offering every employee a "free gym membership," but wellness is obviously so much more as I've stated in this chapter. Promoting a culture of wellness is not a "check off the box" action that a leader takes, but rather a frame of mind and a value system that is established, revised, implemented, and reinforced every day. Let's get well...together.

Chapter 16

"The Great Resignation"...
It's Not Personal. (Or Is It?)

Some say that when a talented and valued team member leaves your organization; "It's not personal." Funny, when people leave a team, it is rare that the departing employee will ever say directly to the team leader; "I just didn't like working for you or being on your team!" Another thing I keep thinking about when it comes to losing talented team members is a quote that just keeps resonating and goes like this; "People don't leave jobs—people leave bosses!" Ouch.

Retaining Your Best People is No Guarantee

Okay...it's time that we talk about some especially tough stuff when it comes to being a leader. Some disclosure is in order. Over the past year, our relatively small organization, tightknit team, has had five team members leave. A few of them were really terrific and key players in our team's success. One of those team members, we will call "Cathy", worked hand in hand with me and Mary helping to make strategic business and fiscal decisions on behalf of our organization. No lie, Cathy's leaving hurt a lot.

In fact, Mary, who is rarely thrown off her even-keel leadership persona, was thrown for a loop when Cathy informed her that she was about to make a move. Says Mary; "I was shaken to the core. Someone who I relied on for so many essential responsibilities for nearly a decade had just given her notice. My mind raced from anger, to sadness, to resentment and then simply to fear, as I realized the daunting task ahead of us of involved not only finding someone to fill Cathy's shoes, but then the process of onboarding him or her. Losing a team member is never easy but losing someone who plays such a critical role in the organization is even more challenging."

Further, especially in the case I just described, it was not only a shock because neither Mary nor I saw it coming, but it caused me as a leader and someone who teaches and coaches in this field to do a lot of soul searching and self-examination.

By way of background, Cathy was receiving a significant salary and it had been increased several times with substantial raises and bonuses for performance along the way. At the time, she said she was "very grateful," especially during these challenging and uncertain times post-COVID. Further, both Mary and I made a point of reinforcing the message that "flexibility" was and is the key aspect to our organizational culture and from our perspective, "family always comes first" especially once COVID-19 became such a significant part of our lives in early 2020. At that time and moving forward, Mary and I made the decision to allow all of our team members to work from home and no matter what family or personal situation arose, that always came first.

Career Choices Are Highly Personal

So, when Cathy told Mary, and then me, about her leaving to pursue an opportunity to work for another non-profit that was directly involved in feeding and servicing people who were homeless, she said this; "It's time for me to do something that has a more direct impact on people's lives—to do my part." Who can argue with that? It appeared to be a highly personal and profound decision on Cathy's part, and I had to respect that and her for caring nearly as much about making a difference in the lives of others less fortunate.

As for our organization, while we work hard producing and broadcasting socially relevant and topical programming on several PBS TV stations that we believe is important, it clearly doesn't compare with helping those who are homeless. I was also confident that the non-profit Cathy was going to was not paying her nearly as much as we were—not to mention her work would no longer be 100% remote, and therefore she would have to travel into the office on a regular basis.

So...what does all this mean when a top team member chooses to make a career change and leave your organization? What does it say about us as leaders and how much we can at least influence our team members and their sense of loyalty to our organization versus seeking potential opportunities on the outside? How much of any of this has to do with us as leaders versus the highly personal decisions people make about their lives and their work? Cathy was emotional when she gave her notice, and she kept telling us that it was "great working with us" and it was in fact "a personal decision" to make a direct impact at a pivotal point at this juncture in her life. It wasn't us; it was Cathy doing what was best for her.

People Leaving...Is It Personal?

Yet, in spite of everything Cathy said—including how much she enjoyed the experience of working with us—I immediately started playing that nagging voice in my head that kept saying, "People don't leave jobs, people leave bosses." Some personal disclosure. I remember growing up and watching my father, Steve Adubato, Sr., leading his not-for-profit organization in Newark, NJ, and the way he reacted when key team members decided to leave his team. His first reaction was to be angry and Steve, Sr. never held back expressing it. He took a team member deciding to leave as a personal afront, as a lack of loyalty. He would often remind the team member of the many things he had "done for them." Sometimes he would offer more money and pressure the team member to stay. My father was very good at guilting people into reversing their decisions and "staying with him" and his organization.

The only problem with that approach was that over time, many of these same team members would ultimately decide to leave my father's organization. He was just so domineering and powerful in what he said and how he said it that his ability to persuade, and yes intimidate people, was profound. I would be lying if I said I wasn't influenced by some of my father's less than admirable leadership traits (and a few of his considerably great leadership traits). No, I was never in your face or confrontational with a team member who wanted to leave. I never tried to guilt or remind people of "what I did for them." But the emotions and feelings of abandonment including "where's the loyalty?" were very much there, and in many ways, still are.

I knew as a leader it was not productive to take Cathy's departure personally. Yet, that is not the same as refusing to look inward and asking yourself some deeply "personal" questions about one's own leadership style and what, if any, impact this may have had on Cathy or any other talented team member leaving. To say that a leader's style has absolutely nothing to do with decisions team members make to leave is often wishful thinking and unrealistic. It must be part of the equation on some level, right? So, while I didn't want to take Cathy's decision personally, that was easier said than done. It is one thing to read and understand on an intellectual level about the "great resignation", but it is quite another when it happens on your watch, on your team, with your best people.

Time For a "Personal" Self-Assessment

And yes, it did start to feel pretty "personal" when another talented, dedicated, twenty-something team member, who we will call "Jane," at our organization said she was leaving our team. This valuable employee told me when pressed on the issue that her decision was largely to pursue an opportunity in a very different field, but part of her decision was because she felt that no matter what she did, that I, as the team leader, would never be satisfied. My first instinct was to explain my leadership style being all about the pursuit of excellence, but instead I chose to listen. At least her feedback and candor could help me as a leader understand my role in her decision and moving forward make some adjustments with other team members. Some background—we hired Jane right out of college. Mary and I worked really hard to develop and coach her and tried our best to create a career path that was challenging and rewarding. Jane was promoted several times into positions with more responsibility. We consistently raised her salary. We decided to put her on camera and coached her in this regard as well. We gave her consistent, and what we felt was constructive feedback. She moved from a purely behind the scenes producer to a combination executive producer, on camera contributor and key member of our organization. All this before the age of 30.

I thought that was what she wanted, and yes, the end of her time with us ended very amicably. In fact, recently, this very talented young professional asked me for a letter of recommendation to a graduate program at a major university that I am affiliated with. I was glad to write it and proud of Jane's trajectory after she left our team. She has a very bright future. But again, you can't be a leadership coach (and write 6 books on the topic of leadership and communication) and not struggle with the question of how and why talented team members leave and what, if anything, we as leaders can and should be doing to keep those players on board and happy and thriving.

What went wrong? Fact is, as I look back at Jane's time with us, on certain occasions (too many in fact), I clearly overreacted and poorly handled things that I perceived had gone wrong. I was too emotional and not strategic or solution oriented. I blamed too often. At times, I just wouldn't let things go. I raised my voice in certain situations and at times contributed to a less than positive work environment. None of this was or is acceptable for any leader—but it was especially troublesome when dealing with Jane—an extremely nice, pleasant and sensitive person who I am sure was put off by some of my actions in what I thought were rare situations. But like one of my favorite axioms says on a large poster in our home, "NO EXCUSES!" I have to own this, which is something I find embarrassing and difficult to face. It is even more challenging to write this in a book on leadership.

With the above examples in mind and considering the talented people on your team who have decided to leave, the following are some important actions and "best practices" that can increase the odds that your best people will want to stay on board—even though there will always be factors beyond your control as a leader.

Stay connected on a regular basis. The goal is to make regular communication with every team member part of your leadership DNA. It is not a check off the box kind of thing. It is keeping it top of mind. Staying engaged. Texting, e-mailing, calling out of the blue, just to see how team members are doing and what issues and/or challenges they may be having. Staying connected is especially more difficult when people don't work in the same office, as is the case with our team, but it is not an excuse to not do it in every way we can.

Read the tea leaves. For leaders that are intuitive and have a high degree of emotional intelligence you should be able to pick up the signs and signals that something is off or wrong with a particular team member. I am not talking about looking for a problem that doesn't exist but listen and observe. It is about tone of voice, body language, a lack of engagement and enthusiasm. Read the tea leaves and deal with it directly with individual team members because hoping things work out isn't really a great plan. People often say, "I'm sure things will work out over time." Sometimes they do, but often things get worse. And hoping and praying only matters when you do your part as a more engaged, proactive leader.

Show me the money. Mary has pushed me over the years to simply pay people more. We pay considerably more for the same position than we did just a few years ago. In many cases I have gone beyond my so-called comfort zone from a fiscal point of view. But, Mary argues, and she is right, that given how many options people have to lead and go where they think the grass may be in fact greener somewhere else, you have got to put up real money. You've got to invest in your people. No, it is not a guarantee that people will stay, but having people leave over "money" in this environment is an unforced error, because the amount of money, time and effort we spend recruiting and training new people costs a heck of a lot more.

Be flexible on virtually everything except the standard of excellence and clear deadlines that must be met in order for your organization and team to meet its goal. Be flexible with hours and when people work and when they take care of other important aspects of their life. Be flexible with where people work so that it is most conducive for them to be as productive and comfortable as possible.

Acknowledge and recognize your people. Great leaders are vigilant in recognizing and celebrating when team members succeed. Send an e-mail about someone kicking butt, not just to them but in some cases the entire team. Text them and tell them "great job" or call them and tell them the same thing. Reward them financially beyond their base salary with bonuses and in some cases salary adjustments for going above and beyond. Again, no guarantee they are going to stay as you have seen from this chapter, but not doing it is simply not smart.

Put people in a position to succeed. Smart leaders identify the key strengths of their team members and put them in the right roles for success. Of course, we need to develop people in areas where they can improve. However, this should not be done by putting them in a position to fail—which will only increase the odds that disappointment and disillusionment will set in.

Lead on a two-way street. It's one thing to communicate specific goals that YOU would like a team member to accomplish, but it is also important that a team member is given the opportunity to tell you what he or she thinks is important. Creating a two-way street with open communication is critical to effective mentoring and coaching.

Stay with it. Even if the team member gets defensive when you deliver hard to hear feedback, it is essential that you communicate that you are being direct, "Because I care about you and your future. The only way you are going to get better is by having hard conversations like this." Stick with it, even if you don't get the reaction you'd like at first. P.S. if a team member leaves because you are giving constructive and useful feedback, it is probably for the best—for both parties.

Invest the time. No matter how busy you are with your day-to-day responsibilities, there is no substitute for spending time with individual team members. It's important that your people know that you care about them and their future.

Variety motivates. If you do the same thing every day, you are going to be unmotivated and disengaged. Conversely, mixing up your professional portfolio is motivating. Smart leaders are constantly looking at a team member's responsibilities and looking for ways to challenge them to get outside their comfort zone—challenging certain team members in this fashion risks turning them off, but do you really want a team member who clings to the status quo?

Be consistent in your expectations. Great leaders communicate to employees exactly what they expect and when their people perform at that level, they are rewarded and recognized. Real employee engagement requires open and honest communication that is consistent and clear. Changing expectations on a whim and sending conflicting messages about goals can be frustrating to a team member.

Be transparent. Share information and communicate about the bigger picture. Too often, leaders don't share important information about where things are heading for fear of employees not being able to handle it. For people to feel engaged, they must be involved, which requires that leaders take the risk of sharing information about where the organization is going and why. It also includes being candid about real organizational challenges, especially in the post-COVID era where the need to adapt and pivot is essential.

Collaborate and involve employees in the decision-making process. You are not expected to have all the answers. Sometimes, as a leader, sharing a difficult question or challenge with employees and asking for their feedback will engage them in identifying a possible solution. This often creates a greater degree of ownership and investment in the team and organization.

Communicate on multiple platforms. It is important that leaders have engaging, interactive and inclusive meetings, but in an age of digital, virtual omnipresent mobile technology, it is essential that leaders who want to connect with employees also use other communication platforms such as Twitter, Facebook and Zoom, as well as e-mail and texting.

Chapter 17
Retire? Why?...I Love My Work!

About a decade ago, I was providing executive leadership and communication coaching at a major accounting firm on the East Coast. The CEO was a very strong leader who had brought me into the firm to "Help develop the next generation of leaders" who he said would "Support me in my retirement."

When "Joe" first told me this, I remember thinking; "Why would this guy retire when he is in his early 60s and he is at the top of his game?" I said this to Joe, and I wasn't just kissing up to a major client, which I am more than capable of doing. I really meant it. Joe was a smart, engaged, strategic leader who had a clear sense about the firm's future and led the effort to merge the firm with other accounting firms. These strategic moves were innovative and impactful. I will never forget his response to my question about why what seemed to me to be his premature retirement strategy; "Steve, I thought you knew that our firm has a mandatory retirement policy. It is 62 and out." Huh? I was stunned and asked what the "logic" was behind such a policy. When I asked as to why 62, Joe responded, "We need to make room for more partners, and we need to promote the younger people at the firm that you will be coaching."

I had a great relationship with this accounting firm for well over a decade coaching and developing the high-potential professionals there—many of whom went on to become partners. Yet, during the more than 10 years consulting and coaching for the firm, I saw many senior equity partners in their early 60s stepping down—forced to retire—because of the firm's "mandatory retirement policy."

Isn't Age REALLY Just a Number?

So here is the deal. Full disclosure, as I write this chapter, I am a little bit past that mandatory retirement age. I keep asking myself, how would I feel if PBS had a policy that said; "Steve, sorry, but you have reached our mandatory retirement age. We just can't have you on the air any longer. We wish you a lot of luck. You're done!"

And, what about if the clients at Stand & Deliver had a policy in which they didn't have "people my age" coaching or training their leaders? The same thing can be said of writing your next book and a publisher saying, "Sorry, we don't have authors who are 62 or over." You get the picture yet? Call me delusional, but I feel and strongly believe that as of this writing, I am at the top of my professional game. I feel more creative, more engaged and strategic, as well as feeling more grounded as a leader than ever. I am convinced that I am better at what I am doing than I was 20 years ago. I am a bit calmer and less reactive. I am more focused on finding solutions than pointing the finger of blame, even though I don't bat 1,000. With age comes experience. With experience comes judgment. With judgment comes improved results.

Further, writing this book about the "tough stuff" is something I believe I am better equipped to do at this stage of my career. I know that 10 or 20 years ago I wouldn't have had the perspective and maturity, as well as the self-awareness and confidence, to write in this way.

Let's explore this topic in more depth. As leaders—as professionals—we work so hard to support our families and try to create the most comfortable lifestyle, preparing for our retirement. I will never forget meeting with our financial advisor about a decade ago and talking about my "retirement plan." The entire discussion centered on "savings" that my wife, Jen, and I would likely have as a monthly spending budget based on retiring at 62 or 64 or, God forbid, 66. But as they say, "that was then..." A decade later, retirement is not something I look forward to or plan on from a professional perspective. Of course, I keep a close eye on our investment portfolio. We have worked to save for college for our three children. I'm also pretty good on the life insurance end of things and I've planned my will. You get the picture...but retire? Why? Why would I retire? Stop working? Stop creating? Stop being productive, learning, growing, innovating, and, hopefully, getting better every day—mistakes and all?

Retirement Is Highly Personal

Like many professionals, I enjoy making money, living a comfortable life, and I am aware of our bottom line. I am very competitive about business development and raising the capital needed to run two successful businesses, employ a solid team of people—especially my colleague of 23-years Mary Gamba—and remain in the black. But I don't work as hard as I do just because of money. Fact is, I simply love my work. I love the challenge, and I also really like to develop new projects as well as coaching and developing team members. And yes, being professionally relevant still matters a lot to me. For me, it's not just "business", it's personal. Am I saying that I want to work at this pace—with the pressures to raise money, secure and keep new clients and sponsors, make payroll, etc.., until I drop? Of course not. In fact, Mary and I have talked and acted, especially in the last few years, to eliminate "unnecessary activity" and focus more on having greater strategic impact. Some projects and initiatives have been eliminated and Mary and I try to take Fridays "off," but we still wind up talking and staying connected to our business, yet taking some time for ourselves. But I do feel energized, creative and can't seem to stop coming up with new and interesting projects and initiatives for our two companies—as well as for myself as a professional and as a leader. I'm not saying everyone who works with me likes or even appreciates that part of my personality, but I am just putting it out there as to why retirement, mandatory or otherwise, feels so foreign to me.

I have a lot of new PBS programming ideas—new ways to run our production company to be more effective and efficient—new content for the leadership academies and seminars Mary and I facilitate through our firm Stand & Deliver. As I write this chapter on "retirement", I taught a "master class" at Seton Hall University to a group of 20 students in which I engaged these kids—four decades younger than me—about the importance of "finding their voice" as leaders by becoming more confident and persuasive public presenters. The students presented and I facilitated the class, giving them candid, yet supportive, feedback. I saw their faces beam with pride when their fellow students applauded after they presented. I enthusiastically led that applause. It was exhilarating, inspiring and fun! I have previously taught a two-day master class at Caldwell University in their doctoral program in education administration for superintendents, principals and other educational administrators. In the class, I challenged these dedicated educational professionals in one-on-one "mock" interviews in which they faced a hypothetical "crisis" or dealt with a challenging or controversial issue. Again, this teaching experience, which trust me I don't do for the money, is professionally and personally rewarding. Most recently, I am returning to my alma mater, Rutgers University, to the Eagleton Institute of Politics where I was a grad student to lead a seminar and do a podcast on "Democracy at a Crossroads" and the importance of public service.

Further, I love facilitating our leadership and communication seminars at Stand & Deliver. I truly love working with Mary as we "co-host" *Lessons in Leadership*, our weekly video podcast. I continue to appreciate seeing Mary grow into a strong, confident on-air partner. I appreciate the way Mary challenges me to think about our work and "life" in ways that are not natural for me. We push each other to be the best version of ourselves. That is exciting. So again, why exactly would I retire?

I really enjoy my executive coaching where I try to help professionals reach their potential as leaders. And clearly, I very much appreciate the work I do as an interviewer on public broadcasting in which I meet fascinating people from all walks of life who are making a difference in the lives of others and dealing with society's most difficult and complex issues. And, as I said, working with each team member at the Caucus Educational Corporation continues to be both challenging and rewarding, including working with a new 24-year-old marketing and social media team member who both Mary and I see great potential in. That's exciting.

So...Am I a Workaholic?

In many ways, yes, I must confess. I'm guilty as charged. But I don't see it as a bad thing to love your work. To be clear, outside of my work, I try to enjoy a range of activities including struggling to become a better golfer and exercising on a regular basis. Peloton and a small home gym have been a blessing. I'm not bragging. I'm just saying that I'm convinced that loving what I do professionally doesn't negatively impact my effort to be a better father, husband, and friend with tons of flaws.

I know, I just shared an awful lot about myself, and it may sound a little self-congratulatory. But, I'm trying to make this point; For some of us, working, including writing this book, my 6th, is pretty joyful. It keeps me sharp. I feel challenged every day and hopefully, just a little bit relevant.

Full disclosure, I have other reasons for not wanting to retire any time soon beyond the fact that I really enjoy the work. This is really "tough stuff" to talk about in this book or anywhere, but my father passed away in the fall of 2020, after nearly a decade of suffering terribly with dementia. Just writing this is causing a range of emotions. My father was a bull of a man. Strong. Tenacious. Relentless. A great public communicator and innovative leader who had tons of flaws, both in his professional and personal life. Yet, watching him deteriorate over the years to the point where he couldn't speak (and my father loved to talk) was devastating to me on a deeply personal level. His favorite expression when he was in "Steve Sr. lecture mode" was "listen to me!"

For anyone reading this, if you have a close family member or friend who has gone through something like this, you know how it plays out. It is horrible. I am haunted by the memory of sitting by my father's bed, with him just staring at me with his eyes glassy. He would often just hold and squeeze my hand. I think he knew it was me, his only son. But who really knows? I just can't imagine how he was feeling, stuck in this never-ending nightmare that he had no control over. Yes, I feel terrible for my mother who cared for my father in ways I still can't comprehend. Yet, for the child of a parent with dementia, at least this particular son, I would be lying to say that I am not deathly afraid of my own mind deteriorating and potentially experiencing some form of dementia. Who knows if it is genetic? What does any of this have to do with retirement and work? Well, everything I've read says you must keep your mind engaged and active. Keep your brain functioning and sharp. Will working prevent dementia? Probably not. But, just like exercising on a regular basis to keep our muscles strong, I've convinced myself that I must do the same thing when it comes to my mind. I may be wrong, but what exactly do I have to lose?

Retirement Isn't Exactly a Black and White Thing

For some leaders and professionals who love what they do, despite the many challenges that inevitably go along with it, retirement can be "very tough stuff." Some of us, no matter how much we love and appreciate our significant other and/or our children, close friends, or hobbies, our work is a huge part of who we are as human beings. For some of us, giving up our work in many ways is a death of sorts. Again, not for everyone, but I know I am not alone in this, and I am also sure that issues of ego, pride, insecurity, and vulnerability are in part tied to my thinking about retirement.

Finally, as I attempt to put this chapter to rest, I think about an in depth 2021 interview I conducted with leadership guru Ken Blanchard, who at the time was 82-years-old. At the time of the interview, I had read every one of Blanchard's books on leadership and I was a huge fan. I still am. He is a giant in the field of leadership. An icon. As he talked about his work and the inspiring message from his book co-authored with Morton Shaevitz called, *Refire! Don't Retire: Make the Rest of Your Life, the Best of Your Life,* Blanchard shared the following, "Take a look at your life in terms of what are you doing to refire yourself intellectually, physically, spiritually, and relationship-wise? I'm just as excited now, as I was forty or fifty years ago - what an exciting time to be alive!"

As I interviewed Ken, I kept thinking, he is is 82. 82! And he is at the top of his game. Sharp. Insightful and full of energy. Selfishly, I thought to myself, this guy has about 20 years on me. Who says I can't be doing what I love for 20 years or more? So, if I am still 'refiring" then why retire? I don't know if I should thank Ken Blanchard or curse him for inspiring and motiving me in this way. While retirement is clearly right for many top-notch professionals, for some of us, we think, retire? Why? Why should I when I still love what I do?

About the Author

STEVE ADUBATO, Ph.D., is a prolific writer. His books include *Speak from the Heart (Simon & Schuster)*, *Lessons in Leadership, What Were They Thinking?*, *Make the Connection*, and *You are the Brand* (all Rutgers University Press). He is an Emmy® Award-winning anchor of programming broadcast on PBS stations Thirteen/WNET and NJ PBS.

Formerly New Jersey's youngest state legislator at the age of 26, Steve also previously served as a distinguished visiting professor on the subject of leadership at New York University, and he has also lectured on the subjects of leadership and communication at the New Jersey Institute of Technology, the United States Military Academy at West Point as well as teaching a Master Class on leadership at the Buccino Leadership Institute at Seton Hall University and the Eagleton Institute of Politics at Rutgers University.

Steve has appeared on NBC's TODAY Show, NPR, CNN, MSNBC, CBS New York, and FOX5 NY as a media and political analyst and is the host of *Steve Adubato's Lessons in Leadership with Co-host Mary Gamba*. His firm, Stand & Deliver, offers leadership workshops and executive coaching for professionals in a variety of industries and organizations.

Thank you for reading.

Please review this book. Reviews
help others find Absolutely Amazing eBooks and
inspire us to keep providing these marvelous tales.
If you would like to be put on our email list
to receive updates on new releases,
contests, and promotions, please go to
AbsolutelyAmazingEbooks.com and sign up.

For sales, editorial information, subsidiary rights information
or a catalog, please write or phone or e-mail
Brick Tower Press
Manhanset House
Shelter Island Hts., New York 11965-0342, US
Tel: 212-427-7139
www.BrickTowerPress.com
bricktower@aol.com
www.IngramContent.com

For sales in the UK and Europe please contact our distributor,
Gazelle Book Services
White Cross Mills
Lancaster, LA1 4XS, UK
Tel: (01524) 68765 Fax: (01524) 63232
email: jacky@gazellebooks.co.uk

Printed in the USA
CPSIA information can be obtained
at www.ICGtesting.com
LVHW021401261023
762144LV00019B/87/J